My Round the World Journal

SAMANTHA SAUNDERS

Copyright © 2015 Samantha Saunders

All rights reserved.

ISBN-13: 978-1505828030
ISBN-10: 1505828031

DEDICATION

I would like to dedicate this book to my wonderful husband Dean for encouraging me to go ahead and write it. If it weren't for his support and encouragement, the words in this journal would still be sitting on mildew-ridden paper somewhere in the loft.

To my parents for making their dream a reality, for sharing it with us, and keeping us safe at all times on this great adventure. To my grandparents and aunt for always supporting me in everything that I do.

Some names have been changed in this book.

CONTENTS

1	It started with a dream	Pg #7
2	The Atlantic Crossing	Pg #11
3	Exploring the Caribbean	Pg #29
4	Caribbean Cruising	Pg #41
5	Saying our Farewells	Pg #59
6	Joining the Rally	Pg #73
7	The Panama Canal	Pg #85
8	Stunning Galapagos	Pg #91
9	The Pacific Crossing	Pg #97
10	French Polynesia	Pg #101
11	The Worst Storm	Pg #109
12	The Land of Oz	Pg #123
13	Towed into Bali	Pg #137
14	Indonesia & Malaysia	Pg #143
15	Thailand	Pg #155
16	Sri Lanka – Land of Tea	Pg #165
17	Magical Maldives	Pg #171
18	Keeping an eye out for Pirates	Pg # 175
19	Conquering the Red Sea	Pg # 179
20	The Suez Canal	Pg # 201
21	Sailing the Med	Pg # 205
22	Madeira	Pg # 231
23	The Canaries	Pg # 239
24	The Atlantic Crossing – Round 2	Pg # 243
25	Back in the Caribbean	Pg # 251
26	A little update	Pg # 253

Chapter 1
It started with a dream

Introduction

Back in 1995, my parents had just sold their business and were getting itchy feet to go travelling with their young family. They had sailed a few times before on various flotilla holidays in the Mediterranean, a few times with a skipper and a few times alone. They started going to various boat shows around the country and soon fell in love with a boat manufacturer called Oyster. They wanted a well-made boat that was ocean going and one that would keep us all safe in heavy seas. That year Oyster happened to be bringing out a brand new 45-footer that had three cabins, two heads (the yachtie terminology for toilets) and was perfect for accommodating our family of five. Along with my parents there were my two younger sisters, Danielle and Corrie-Anne, and me, Samantha.

Before we knew it the boat was being designed and built and was being shown in the Southampton boat show where we all went to see it finished for the first time. She looked beautiful. My sisters and I were so excited running through the boat trying out the bunks in each cabin and pretending to cook in the kitchen. At that time it was hard to imagine that we would soon be sailing around the world on her.

Rainbow Spirit at Southampton BoatShow 1995

My parents were pretty environmentally friendly. In their earlier life they had spent several months trekking through the rainforests of Borneo trying to stop the deforestation and logging there, as well as setting up a mail order company in the UK selling sustainable and environmentally friendly products. So the environment was very close to their hearts and they wanted to give the boat an earthy name. We pondered on the name "Disappearing World" for a while, but we all thought that was a little too depressing, I mean what if the boat disappeared or something. We finally settled on the name Rainbow Spirit, inspired by the Greenpeace boat Rainbow Warrior.

UK to the Canaries

My parents and middle sister Dani set sail from the UK for the first time in 1995. They sailed straight out of Ipswich, across the Bay of Biscay and arrived in the Canaries a few weeks later. They decided to take a delivery skipper with them on this initial trip. This was so the skipper could show them the ropes of handling a larger boat from what they were previously used to. It was a good job that he was there because midway across the Biscay they hit a huge storm with 60-foot seas. To this day they were the biggest seas my parents have encountered sailing. Even the delivery skipper was nervous, but as the waves were extremely far apart the seas were more like a very high swell.

Samantha Saunders

Chapter 2
The Atlantic Crossing

The Atlantic Crossing

The first proper voyage for me on the boat was the Atlantic Crossing. This time my parents decided to take me on this leg of the trip and as they now felt comfortable enough sailing the boat by themselves it meant they no longer needed a skipper.

We decided to join a sailing fleet called Arc (Atlantic Rally for Cruisers), which was an organisation that had been running it every year since 1986. Every year hundreds of boats prepared to leave on the long transatlantic voyage to the Caribbean supporting each other along the way and staying in touch daily via radio.

The starting point was Las Palmas, Grand Canaria, in the Canaries and we spent the two weeks before we left preparing the boat for the crossing. We made several trips to the local supermarkets loading more than six large trolleys with provisions each time. Every piece of fruit and vegetable that we brought onboard had to be hand washed and dried on deck before it was taken down below to be stored. We didn't want to bring any critters onboard like cockroaches as we heard that they were a nightmare to get rid of once they were onboard. We stored what we could in the various cupboards around the boat. We filled the higher cupboards in the cabins with lighter items like toilet roll and cereals and kept the heavy items towards the bottom of the boat and under the floorboards. The more we brought onboard the heavier the boat became and the lower it sat in the water.

It was tradition that the yachts painted their boat and name on the harbour wall so one day Dad picked up some sample pots of wall paints from the local DIY store and I got to work. The whole harbour wall was covered in yacht paintings from years before. Some were so old the paint had nearly all come off. I painted our boat name in bright colours surrounded by a dolphin and rainbow.

Oyster the boat manufacturer flew out to check any of their boats in the fleet and to offer repairs and support before we set off on our three-week trip. They hosted a cocktail party ashore for the Oyster boats so we got to meet other boat owners. Some were on 90-footers, twice the size of our boat.

24th November 1996

It was the day of setting off. One by one each boat left the marina and circled the bay, waiting for the start of the race. There were around 140 of us setting sail. The boats ranged in size from 30 to 100-foot and there were crews from all corners of the globe including families and couples. So many people turned up to wave us off, the promenade was full of waving spectators and the harbour was full of support boats. Everyone was blowing their hand held and boat horns. I was in charge of our horn but it was one of those pump up ones so it only blasted for about 10 seconds before it had to be pumped up again. Most of the other boats had a built in electric horn, which could blast endlessly.

Suddenly there was a loud bang, a cannon was fired from a nearby Spanish naval ship to mark the beginning of the race and we were off. It was exciting knowing that we were about to embark on a three-week crossing with all of these other boats, but also rather scary knowing that in a few days we would soon lose sight of them as we would all be travelling at different speeds and soon we would be sailing by ourselves.

Rainbow Spirit at the start of the race, and Dad at the helm

All the boats at the start line

That night as we sailed further away from land, it started to get more and more choppy and the seasickness started to kick in. I had never experienced seasickness before but I guess I hadn't really been on too many boats either. Mum also felt a little queasy so Dad helped out by cooking dinner down below. He didn't seem to feel the sickness at all so he sent me to bed for an early night. As darkness came around, the moon came out and the yachts in the distance turned to little white bobbing lights on the horizon.

25th November 1996

Dad thought it was time that I had the responsibility of taking my own watches during the day so he and mum could get some rest. There always had to be someone on deck on the look out for other ships and boats and even debris in the water that could cause a collision. You also had to keep an eye out for changing weather conditions and any squalls that could catch you out at any minute. The wind had to be in the sails constantly and as the wind was very unpredictable and changed direction by the hour, you had to constantly adjust the sails to suit. When the wind picked up we took some sail in and if the wind speed fell then we were able to put more sail out to help catch more breeze.

Squalls were masses of cloud, which usually brought heavy rain, and 9 times out of 10 they brought increased wind. Sometimes wind speeds picked up from a comfy 15 knots to over 35 knots and the boat leaned to one side as it gently tried to tip the wind out of its sail and the boat speed increased. Then the rain usually hit, making visibility quite poor. I didn't like the squalls as they were too unpredictable and I certainly didn't like it when the boat leaned right over, but some only lasted a few minutes and by the time we had all rushed on deck and took some sail in the squall had already passed.

As I was only 11 years old, Dad started me off on a few day watches until I got used to it. He gave me three hours in the morning from 7am-10am, two hours after lunch from 2pm-4pm and then three hours just before bedtime from 8pm to 11pm. During my morning watch Mum came on for an hour with me, helping me to settle in and set me up for my two hours alone. Then in the evening Dad joined me for an hour, so it was a nice way to spend some quality time with them individually.

We had been at sea for less that 24 hours now and I was still feeling queasy. I found going up on deck helped. Having fresh air in your face and being able to focus your eyes on the water made everything seem better.

In the evening it was time to tune into the local SSB Radio and report our daily position to the other yachts. There was someone in charge taking everyone's positions and marking the progress of each yacht, but when we tried to tune in on the first evening, our SSB radio wasn't working. The SSB (single side band) allowed us to communicate with other boats hundreds of thousands of miles away. We had another radio called a VHF (very high frequency) but the communication distance for this was only usually around the line of sight, so around 15-40 miles or so. As soon as we were more than this distance away from another yacht, there was no way to communicate with anyone. It dawned on us that in a few days when the distance grew between each boat that we really would be by ourselves. It was a little scary thinking that we still had another three weeks to go and there would be times that if something did happen or we got into trouble and needed help that we were alone and unable to contact anyone.

On the bright side, the weather was quite calm, my seasickness had passed and we were now averaging around 6 knots, which was good. Now 6 knots for all those non-yachties is just less that 7mph, now that's pretty slow compared to a car. It's like gentle jogging speed, but now you know why it takes over three weeks to travel around 3000 miles across the Atlantic Ocean.

Me taking the helm on my watch

During the evening just into my 8pm watch, I saw my first shooting star. I almost thought my eyes were playing up at first, I couldn't believe it. I had never seen one before and thought it was amazing. That night I saw another five and each one lasted only a few seconds. They were all bright yellow and orange and before you could blink they were gone. Some shot through the sky high up in all directions and some appeared to be falling into the water on the horizon.

26*th* November 1996

As my morning watch was coming to an end a school of dolphins decided to join the boat. There must have been at least 20 and they were swimming all around the boat at the same speed as us. A few took to the bow and swam right in the wake of the bow wave. They seemed to be using the boat as an object to push them along. They jumped in and out of the waves playing with each other. They must have been quite a small breed because they only seemed to be about a metre long.

Dad still couldn't get the SSB to work so he focused his attention on fishing instead. We had never fished from the boat before so we were all rather excited to see what we would catch. He fixed a fishing reel to one of the vertical stainless post rails on the back of the boat and added a very small pink rubber squid as bait. He let the line out about 50 metres or so and waited patiently. By the time it started to get dark we had had no bites so he decided to leave it out for the night. What a huge mistake that was! Around 2am during Dad's watch, something bit the line causing it to click and pull out like mad. Dad took some sail in to slow the boat down and started to slowly bring the line in. As it got nearer and he was able to get his first glimpse of the fish, he realised it wasn't quite what he was expecting. It looked nothing like a fish; it looked more like a snake. He didn't know what to do with it, we sure weren't going to eat it, but we had to get the fish on deck to get the hook and lure out of its mouth. By the time he brought it in the fish had already drowned from being dragged in the water for too long. It turned out to be a very long black, thin, eel-like fish with two devil fangs at the front. We couldn't identify it in our fish book so we didn't know what it was or whether we could even eat it, but it was so ugly that I don't think we would of anyway. We decided to call it the devil fish and to this day we never ever did try to fish at night again.

Dad with the devil fish and me with our first proper catch, a dorado

27th November 1996

After last night's meeting with the devil fish, Dad put the line back out during the day and within a few hours we had another bite. This time it was a beautiful looking fish around two feet long with a large head. Again we had no idea what it was. When it was dying it changed colour from green to yellow and then back to green and we wondered whether this fish could also be poisonous. After looking through a few books we realised that it was the well-known dorado fish. It's also called the Dolphin fish because of its bulbous head, although it's not related to the dolphin. We were so proud of ourselves and of course we had to take photos of our first fish, or shall we say first edible fish.

It was the first time I had picked up a fish before and my gosh was it slimy, smelly and just so fishy, I didn't really want to hold it at all. I kind of stood there holding as little of it as possible, just holding the tail in the tips of my finger, keeping it as far from me as possible, holding my nose while the photo was quickly taken. Dad then had the lovely job of gutting it and cutting it up before we cooked it for dinner. You really can't get much fresher than that can you.

28th November 1996

We managed to get in touch with another boat on the VHF radio during the morning. It was the first communication we'd had with anyone else since setting off. The other boat was half a day ahead of us so we couldn't see them on the horizon, but as we were a bigger and slightly faster boat we would probably end up passing them in the next few days.

We had now been at sea for more than four days and I was starting to get my sea legs. The queasiness has gone and I could now go down below whenever I wanted without feeling ill. As we all slowly got used to the weather and the Atlantic winds kicking in, we were able to get into a routine. We spent a few hours cleaning the boat, freshening up the place and I put my head down to catch up on schoolwork. The high school I attended in the United Kingdom had set me work to do so now that I had my sea legs I could sit downstairs and use the main saloon (living room) table to do some catching up.

I was still struggling a little with my watches. I was pretty lucky that my watches were only during the day and not in the middle of the night but I wasn't used to going to bed so late. For an 11 year old 11pm was pretty late when you had to be up at 7am, and with the boat rocking and rolling and having to get used to all the strange creaks and moans of the boat at night, it was impossible to sleep straight through. It took me at least a week to get used to it, but my body soon adapted to its new sleeping patterns.

29th November 1996

Today the wind picked up a little and as the wind picked up so did the seas. It was definitely more of a challenge to move around the boat. Luckily there were lots of handles inside to hold on to as you moved from room to room. There were also handles on some interior walls and the saloon table and all the shelves had a lip to stop things flying off and were also a good place to grab onto. There were stainless handrails fixed around the deck you could grab onto when you went on deck.

We ended up catching up with the boat we were in touch with yesterday and we could now see them on our horizon. It was quite nice to think that we had company out there and we didn't feel quite as lonely.

Any fresh bread that we had bought in Grand Canaria had either been eaten or was past its sell by date by now, so it was time to bake our first loaf. Mum and I had never done this before, but luckily we had a ready-made mixture that you just added water to. Mum read out the instructions from the back of the package while I got to work on my first ever loaf of bread. A few hours later it was cooked and ready to eat. Fresh bread never tasted so good. It was still warm when we ate it so the butter just melted on it. We decided to eat lunch in the cockpit for a change. Fresh bread, a selection of meats and cheeses, tinned potatoes, which were surprisingly tasty, and some fresh salad.

We still had fresh fish left so we had that for dinner.

30th November 1996

Last night the wind picked up even more. Dad and Mum reefed the sails before they went to bed. Even with the sails pulled in we were still averaging over 7 knots so we were making good progress. The seas were a little choppier, but that was okay as it seemed to make me more alert on my watches.

I had got into a little routine of writing poems on my watches at night to help pass the time. I was in my own little world trying to think of rhyming words when all of a sudden there was a huge bang which jolted the boat and shook the rigging. I had no idea what it was as it was dark, but the boat immediately picked up speed. You could feel the force of the sails pulling on the rigging and making them creak. My heart started to race and Dad immediately shot up the saloon stairs from down below. He quickly spotted that the reefed headsail had somehow fully unfurled itself and was no longer reefed. He quickly grabbed the furling line to pull it in, but there was no tension on the line at all. He kept pulling and suddenly the other end appeared in his hand. It had snapped off so there was now no way to reduce or reef the sail. Unfortunately there was nothing we could do until the morning as it was too dark and dangerous to go on deck to try and sort out the problem. The wind was already gusting over 30 knots and it would have been nice to get some sail in but we just had to push through the night until light came.

As soon as the sun came up Dad went on deck to investigate what had happened. Running down each side of the boat from the bow to stern were bright yellow safety lines which you clipped onto whenever you wanted to go on deck or leave the cockpit. Dad, as usual, clipped on with the line attached to his life jacket before going on deck. This line was a safety precaution and meant that if he did fall overboard he would still be attached to the boat.

On inspecting the broken line he found that the end of the furling line was fixed to the furling gear via a tiny knot that had been sealed by thread. Somehow the thread had broken and the line had popped out. He redid the knot and sewed it up really well so that it would not do it again. We immediately took some sail in and were relieved to have it reefed again in such strong winds. Wow what a stressful and scary night we'd had. I don't think any of us slept much.

Now I really thought that mum would have used all the fish up by now, I think she had been stashing it the freezer. So as usual we had fish for dinner again. I was getting rather sick of it, but luckily we still had some lovely fresh bread left over to help it go down.

Dad and Mum on deck fixing the furling gear

1st December 1996

The newly fixed furling line seems to be holding up nicely. Dad is feeling pretty tired after being up for most of the night before worrying about the sail, so I take over a watch for him while he gets some sleep. We were averaging 8 knots so were making good progress but then we got a weather warning message come through about a severe weather depression directly ahead of us. If we continued along our current route we would end up heading straight into it, so we immediately took action and decided to change angle to avoid it. The new angle allowed us to travel further south and would hopefully mean we would miss the worst of it.

2nd December 1996

The wind instrument decided to play up today. We now had no idea what the wind speed was or what direction it was coming from. Instead we had to guess and adjust the sails to suit. The wind seemed to be coming from directly behind us and so did the seas. This was a good thing because at least it was not hitting us side on. However, when it's behind, we tended to rock from side to side, so I started to feel a bit seasick again.

We decided to put the headsail pole up to help hold the sail out more so it could catch more wind. This was positioned on the forward side of the mast and was connected to the mast at one end, while the other end acted like an arm holding and pushing out the sail. We hadn't done this many times before so it took us a while to figure out what we were doing and to get the lines on. One line was attached to the end holding the pole up, while two other lines attached it to the stern and bow. We could then control it from the cockpit if we wanted, pulling it back towards the cockpit or away from us.

While I was on watch I came up with a little idea. I decided to write some letters on the computer downstairs, print them out and then place them in empty glass bottles to throw overboard. I printed out 15 so I hope Mum and Dad hurry up and drink some more wine to free up some more bottles. The letter was quite short, introduced myself, explained about my trip across the Atlantic and it asked the finder to write back to me and let me know where they found my bottle.

3rd December 1996

Today we had officially passed the half way mark and so far we had travelled 1367 miles. I was feeling pretty tired as I think the watches and lack of quality sleep were catching up with me. We had been at sea for more than 10 days already and I still hadn't completely got over my queasiness. The wind was picking up a little more as we neared the bad weather system and so were the seas so it was making the boat more uncomfortable to go down below.

Mum and Dad surprised me with a little present to mark the half way point. It was a lovely stamp album with several stamp sets to get me started. Dad had also bought a present for mum. Lisa Clayton's single handed round the world journal. Dad said it was for their next adventure, which made Mum laugh.

4th December 1996

Dad must have been tired today because he was supposed to come on watch at 10am to take over from me but he was still in bed. He was normally up and pottering around the boat each morning at 9am, but on this morning I let him sleep in a little longer.

It had been a few days since we had had any fish for dinner and I think Dad was already getting withdrawal symptoms because he decided to put the fishing line out. Within a few hours we heard a bite (high pitched clicking) but when we brought the line in, the lure was gone. The steel cable connecting the nylon fishing line to the lure had been bitten straight through. At over USD$30 a lure Dad didn't want to lose another one so he doubled up the steel wire, added a brand new lure and put the line back out. This time within 15 minutes we had another bite. We took in all the sails, put the boat in reverse so we could get some slack on the line, and slowly reeled the line in. It looked huge under the water, it must have been bigger than me. As we pulled it in nearer the back of the boat, suddenly it got loose and swam away. I think we had allowed the line to have so much slack that the tiny hook had come unhooked from the fish's mouth.

We had already lost two fish today, so we decided to have one more try before we called it a day. Third time lucky they say. We put the line back out and soon enough we had another bite and brought in a beautiful large dorado fish. It took us at least an hour to get it in because this time we decided not to slow the boat down or take the sails in. By the time we had brought the fish in it was completely still so it must have drowned from being dragged through the water for an hour.

Dad leaning down trying to grab the fish with his hands

5th December 1996

We could really feel the temperature changing as we slowly travelled further south and got nearer to the equator. It really was starting to feel warmer during the day and even on the night watches we were wearing fewer layers.

The seas were still rough and it was gusting over 30 knots, that's a force 7 to 8, but that didn't stop Dad going down below to write some postcards. I don't think he suffers from seasickness at all.

6th December 1996

This was our 12th day at sea today and I think we are all starting to get a little bored. Overnight the seas calmed down to a force 5-6 so it was now blowing a nice steady 20-25 knots. The seas were still quite rough, they normally took a day to return to the current wind speed, but it was now okay to go down below and watch a movie. It's been so long since we were able to watch TV down below that we pretty much watched TV for the whole day. It certainly made the watches go more quickly though.

My Round the World Journal

Me filling in the logbook with our position

7*th* December 1996

Our supply of fresh fish had run out so Dad put out the fishing line again. When we got a bite we knew it was something very big, the reel had never screamed so much. For more than an hour we very slowly reeled it in but we couldn't quite make out what it was as it didn't rise to the surface like the other fish did, it stayed deep down below. It was almost at the stern when we got our first glimpse of it. It looked massive and had a pointy snout. We recognised it as a sailfish because of its long fin on top. It was so big we really had no idea how to get in onboard. It was far too big for a net or for Dad to grab it. After contemplating what to do Dad came up with the idea of slipping a noose around and down the line, slipping it over the fish's body, and tightening it up at its tail. That way we could lift the fish up from its tail and secure it to the back of the boat. We finally got it onto the bathing platform at the back of the boat and Dad held tightly onto the line from the deck above. The fish began to shake so much that the hook and lure flew out of its mouth so we really couldn't afford to let go of the rope now. It banged and shook so violently against the life raft that we started to worry that it would set it off. We decided to put alcohol down its gills to try and stun it and it seemed to do the job. After looking in our fish book we discovered that it was a blue marlin. It was the biggest fish we had caught to date and measured 63 inches long (5'3" long.). That was taller than me.

After taking some proud photos Dad gutted it and cut it up into nice large steaks. We tossed the head and tail overboard and notice a suckerfish about a foot long, attached to the underside of its belly. There is no way we would be able to eat all of this between the three of us....well not unless we had it for breakfast and lunch as well.

10*th* December 1996

The seas have finally calmed down, they seemed so gentle now. Mum is so engrossed in her new Lisa Clayton book that she can't put it down. She loves reading.

Mum chilling in the cockpit with her new book

12*th* December 1996

We had a little visitor today. We spotted a bird on the side rail. He must have been so tired because he kept nodding off. Who knows how long he had been at sea for?

My Round the World Journal

Our little visitor

We take a look at our ETA (estimated time of arrival) and it has us arriving at 10pm tonight. We decide that we really don't want to navigate in the dark so we take in all the sails and slow right down to about 3 knots. This delays our ETA to the early hours of the next morning, a much more suitable time to enter through unknown areas.

13*th* December 1996

The sun started to come up at 6am and we got our first glimpse of landfall. Saint Lucia looked very lush and green. In another hour or so we will finally be on dry land again after being at sea for 19 days. As we near land the wind dies down and we take in the sails and pole we have out and motor towards out next waypoint. But as we near land it seems like we are headed straight for it. This didn't feel right and so we quickly disable the autopilot, take the helm and turned the boat 90 degrees to the right, before we get any closer. Dad went down below to see what was going on and noticed that we had missed the waypoint around the headland and instead we were on course straight through the land as the marina was on the other side. He reset it and we motored around the headland to Rodney Bay marina. Gosh it's a good job we were on deck to notice.

As we entered Rodney Bay we passed a yellow flag to the starboard side, marking the finish line. As soon as we arrived into the marina everyone starts cheering and blasting horns. What a welcome! We were met by a huge crowd of people and as soon as we were docked we were given a beautiful big basket of local tropical fruits and flowers, a bottle of champagne and a large bottle of local rum.

That night we got to experience our first ever live Caribbean steel pan band and some freshly made rum punch. I didn't realise it was rum punch at first, it tasted like a nice fruit juice. After my second cup it suddenly hit me. I started to feel rather unwell and dizzy, I had no idea what was going on but mum explained that it was the effects of the alcohol. It was a rather scary experience, but luckily mum knew what to do and took me straight back to the boat and fed me bread and water.

We spend the next week welcoming in the last remaining yachts in to the marina, attending yachting events and collecting awards and prizes organised by the Arc staff. One boat came in completely dismasted, I guess their rigging couldn't take the strong winds of the Atlantic. The last boat arrived around 10 days after everyone else, it was also one of the smallest boats to join the race and what a welcome they got, nearly every crew off every yacht stood on the dock welcoming them in. One of the yachties even played a tune on his saxophone as the boat moored up.

23rd December 1996

Ten days later we made the trip to the airport to collect my two younger sisters. Corrie was 8 and Dani was 11 and they had flown in by themselves from England. I had missed them so much. It had been nice having quality time with Mum and Dad but I certainly missed the company of having my sisters around. As soon as they came through the airport doors I ran straight to them and gave them the most humongous hug.

Chapter 3

Exploring the Caribbean

27*[th]* *December 1996*

We finally set sail for the next port. It was only a few hours sail away and the weather was lovely. It was a little anchorage called Marigot Bay with lots of little bars, a beautiful beach and the local hotel there had a swimming pool that was free for us to use. The bay was surrounded by steep forested hills on the three sides. Marigot Bay was famous because the original 'Dr. Doolittle' was filmed here in the 1960s and it was also well known for a number of battles between the French and British navies in the 18th Century. On one occasion the British admiral hid his fleet here from the French by tying palm leaves to the masts to disguise them as palm trees. The French sailed past the bay thinking that nothing was there except palms.

The bay was so pretty and scenic that we ended up staying here for three nights. My sisters and I took full advantage of the free swimming pool and spent our days practising our snorkelling and swimming skills by fetching rocks from the bottom of the pool.

30th December 1996

The next port of call was Anse Chastanet. Instead of anchoring here, we picked up a mooring that prevented our anchor from damaging the local corals. Unfortunately there was a north swell coming right into the anchorage and we rolled and rocked the whole day and night. It was so roly that we decided to head to shore to check out the beautiful beach. The beach was stunning and clean and we had a little snorkel around and we saw so many different fish. We saw trumpet fish, boxfish, angel fish, parrot fish and even some scary looking barracudas. We noticed one of the Arc boats had pulled in on another mooring with four playful boys onboard all similar ages to us, so we played on the beach with them all afternoon, making sandcastles and playing tag.

31st December 1996

By the morning the swell hadn't eased so we decided to move along to the next bay called Soufriere. This was more protected from the northerly swell and instead of anchoring in the bay, we dropped anchor and put our stern to the shore by attaching two long lines to the palm trees there. Soufriere had a small town with lots of little shops and the locals seemed really nice and friendly. The bay was so quiet and peaceful that we decided to spend New Year's Eve here instead, away from the crowds.

3rd January 1997

The next port of call was Jalousie Bay, right between the famous Pitons, which were two steep, volcanic, pyramid-looking mountains.

Towards the northern part of the bay was a very large abandoned hotel. No one was there except for a couple of security guards, but we walked around the premises anyway. The pool was empty and dirty and the hotel and the hotel's beach were deserted and rundown.

We occupied ourselves with some snorkelling and the fish and corals were stunning. This place was even quieter than the last bay. The only bit of life there was a tiny local restaurant called 'bang between the Pitons', because it was literally bang between the Piton Mountains. The restaurant was owned by the well-known Lord Glenconner and the food there was super yummy. We were served by this super chirpy and happy waitress, which made our night. The meal was followed by some local acrobatic twin performers, which were rather good. The restaurant was Indian inspired and there was a local shop attached to the restaurant that was full of trinkets and clothing from India. The items were beautiful but very expensive. Apparently they had even had an elephant on site at one time.

5th January 1997

Today was my birthday. For a surprise we sailed around to the next bay where Dad took us all out to a hotel restaurant to eat. He bought me a brand new snorkelling mask and some flippers. Until now we had been sharing mum's mask so it was nice to have my own. The hotel's beach was beautiful and well looked after. It looked like a resort hotel that we probably shouldn't have been using but the hotel didn't seem to mind.

I couldn't wait to try out my new snorkelling gear so we went snorkelling. Me, Dani and Corrie even did some crab catching. We didn't hurt them. We just caught them, put them in a container and then freed them again afterwards.

6th January 1997

It was time to leave the country of Saint Lucia. We had already been here for a few weeks and with only three months left before we had to return back to the UK we still had so many islands to explore. Every bay we had anchored in Saint Lucia, we had to pay a fee to overnight there so it was also getting expensive.

We decided to head to the island of Saint Vincent and the Grenadines. Saint Vincent was a similar size to Saint Lucia, just a lot more unspoilt, less populated and less touristy. We bypassed Saint Vincent, due to the remote anchorages and lack of civilisation in them, so instead headed to the first Grenadine island directly south of Saint Vincent called Bequia.

As we sailed into Bequia's largest western bay called Admiralty Bay, we were spoilt for choice on where to anchor. The bay was huge, full of yachts and was surrounded by three beautiful white sand beaches. The little island's capital Port Elizabeth was buzzing with people. There were lots of shops, bars and restaurants. We all loved this little place, especially the beautiful beaches. The locals were laid back and friendly and there were quite a few yachties ashore exploring.

10th January 1997

Dad had read in one of his sailing books that Canouan was another beautiful island that we should explore, so we picked up anchor and sailed south to the next Grenadine Island. This island wasn't as busy as Bequia but the beaches were even prettier.

We took a half day hike to the eastern part of the island. There were several beaches on the windward side but they were protected by a huge 3 km reef so were calm. The sand was clean and white and beaches went on into the distance for miles. They looked like something off a postcard and we had it all to ourselves.

When we returned to the boat that evening we noticed that a local wooden yacht had somehow drifted and got stuck on the reef behind. Over the course of the day, the waves slowly knocked it about and it slowly sank. The next day there was nothing left but few bits of wood. We couldn't believe how much damage the waves had done to it overnight.

12th January 1997

The next island on route was Mayreau, one of the tiniest Grenadine islands. As we sailed into Salt Whistle Bay anchorage our eyes lit up. This had to be the best beach so far. How could each place keep getting better? The water was crystal clear and so clean. You could clearly see the sand and rocks on the seabed from the bow of the boat. It was pure paradise.

After a day of swimming and lazing around on the beautiful beach we decided to explore the town centre of Mayreau which was located on the other side of the island. The only way to get there was on foot, over a steepish hill and down the other side. There was no path, just loose rock and soil that had been worn away from the locals walking the same route for years. We passed local goats with their young kids and an old church at the top.

The town centre was pretty small, dotted with a couple of hotels and local bars and restaurants. We found a local restaurant owned by a local rastafarian. He was super friendly and the fish meal that we had there was delicious. Opposite the restaurant we found a gorgeous small puppy tied up so we played with it for a while. When it was time to go home we really didn't want to leave it but it wasn't skinny so we knew it was well looked after.

We all fell in love with this beautiful anchorage so much that we did not want to leave. Mum and Dad were happy chilling and we girls kept ourselves occupied swimming and playing on the beach all day.

17th January 1997

We ended up staying a week in Salt Whistle Bay. It was by far our favourite place so far, but we did need to get a move on, so we lifted our anchor and headed to the next island called Union. We had to navigate through dangerous reefs and marked buoys to get into the anchorage there. It was crowded and it took a while to find a safe spot. It was also very windy, although the sea was calm as reefs and land surrounded us in all directions.

It took us several attempts to anchor as we kept dragging, so we decided not to overnight here but instead dinghy ashore to take a quick look at the local town of Clifton and to check the boat out of the country at customs.

Clifton was dotted with tiny shops, a range of restaurants, a small airport and a few little bars. There was a hotel at the front which sold fresh lobster and had a contained walled area full of slow moving brown nurse sharks you could view. They were bottom feeders so were harmless to humans. They weren't there for us to eat; they were pets for the hotel guests and tourists to look at. They must have been hot in the water though because it was only about half a metre deep and the sun was so strong.

After checking out of the country at the local immigration and customs office, we then upped anchor and headed towards the next visible island, which belonged to the country of Grenada.

Dad carefully navigated us out of the channel between the nasty looking reefs and an hour later we were anchored in Hillsborough Bay on the island of Carriacou.

As soon as we arrived we all went straight ashore for Mum and Dad to check into the country. It was a rather long process and seemed to take quite a while because it was rather busy. If they were lucky and it wasn't busy, they could be in and out within 20 minutes, but today there was a long queue and it took hours.

Now Dad's hair hadn't been cut for many months and it had taken on a very wind swept look and was getting rather long. In fact it had gotten so long that Dad ended up chatting with a local there about getting his hair braided. In the end he decided not to go ahead with it. Maybe he thought he would look rather silly, or maybe he was just joking all along about getting hair braids.

The other Arc boat with the four lads on pulled into the bay so that evening we all went out for a meal. The hotel we ate at had lots of tortoises (land turtles as the locals called them) contained in a walled garden. We found these really interesting so we spent most of the night watching them, picking them up and trying to feed them.

18th January 1997

Last night the boys' parents told Mum and Dad about a tropical island not far from where we were which you could anchor off. It was so small that no one lived there and you could walk around it in about two minutes. It just consisted of pure white sand with a few palm trees. It sounded amazing so we motored to this special island known as Sandy Island. There were only a few boats there and we pretty much had the island to ourselves again. We jumped straight in the dinghy and went exploring. We played games and built turtles in the sand.

The plan was to spend the night here and explore the island the next day again, but towards the evening the wind picked up and the boat started dragging. We re-anchored several times but it would not hold so we quickly motored back to Carriacou before it got dark.

28th January 1997

We now had one of my Dad's good friends from the UK onboard. He was supposed to come in a few days earlier but he kept missing his flight and there was no way to contact him except to turn up at the airport each day and hope he was there. On the third day he finally showed up and we took him back up north to the Grenadine islands. Now that we knew which islands were the prettiest we took him to our favourite anchorages and bays.

On this particular night we headed back to the island of Canouan where we took a mooring buoy instead of anchoring. It was rather windy and as we weren't having the best of luck with anchoring recently, and we were all heading ashore that night, we decided to take the safer option of attaching the boat to a mooring instead. By now we had become experts in setting our anchor alarm on our GPS (Global Positioning System). This gave us the exact position of the boat at all times that we could then mark out on the chart and check our position. Now the GPS had an anchor alarm, which allowed us to save the current anchored position, then if for some reason the boat moved more than about 30 metres from the marked position, an alarm would sound. This had worked great previously and instantly alerted us if we were dragging. On this particular occasion we decided to set it anyway just to be safe.

At around 8am the next morning Dad happened to be having a cup of tea at the navigation table and pondering where we were sailing to next, when suddenly the alarm sounded. The GPS told us we were 50 metres from our set position. Dad looked out of the saloon windows and suddenly noticed that the boats which had been on moorings either side of us were now very far ahead of us. He quickly ran on deck and shouted, "Start the engine". The mooring had broken and we were drifting closer and closer to the reef behind. We were hesitant at first to motor forward in case the lines from the broken mooring were dragging under the boat and got wrapped around the propeller, but on running up to the bow we noticed there were no lines at all. The mooring had snapped off at the top of the chain leaving it attached to our bowlines. We quickly freed our lines from the barnacle encrusted mooring and motored away from danger. This time we anchored. We were all a bit shook up for a while thinking about what would of happened if it had broken a few hours earlier while we were all ashore. It took us back to a few weeks previously when we saw a local yacht get washed up on the exact same reef and within a matter of days there was nothing left of it. We wondered if it had been attached to the same lot of moorings we were on.

When the hotel came around that afternoon to take the fee for using their mooring they were rather embarrassed when we told them that we nearly lost our boat on the reef and refused to pay. We never took a mooring from that hotel again.

1st Feb 1997

Today we sailed to the Tobago Cays, a tiny group of uninhabited islands surrounded by reefs and part of a protected national park. It was well known for its great snorkelling and diving so we had to check it out.

As we entered through the marked channel we passed piles of what looked like pink stones. As we neared them we realised they were large empty conch shells. The conch (Lambi) was a local meat that the locals ate. We had previously eaten it on one of the islands and it tasted quite nice, like a chewy crab/lobster, but was a lot cheaper than lobster.

As soon as we dropped anchor we dinghied towards the reef which was dotted with about 50 little mooring buoys about 50 metres or so apart from each other. They were used for tying the dinghy off onto while you swam and snorkelled in the area.

My dad's friend Dave from the UK was still with us and he and Dad went off snorkelling together while I took a rest in the dinghy and bathed in the warm sun. Suddenly I heard someone shout, "Quickly, help me." It was Dave. He had cramp in his leg and couldn't swim and was struggling to stay afloat. He kept shouting, "Quickly, I need picking up." I didn't know what to do as I had only used the outboard motor on the dinghy a couple of times and Dad had always started it for me. I started pulling frantically on the cord to start it. Dave was panicking now and his shouting was getting louder as he now had cramp in both legs. By this time Dad had heard the shouting but he was quite far away so he quickly started swimming back to the dinghy. I was still pulling the cord trying to get it started but was having no luck. What I didn't realise was that the fuel was turned off. I gave up with the engine, freed the boat from the mooring and started rowing towards Dave who was now drifting further away each second as the current carried him away. It was impossible to row against the strong wind, I wasn't moving at all. I couldn't stop rowing because the wind would have taken the dinghy and I would have been gone, so instead I continued rowing into the wind to maintain my position. Dad had now reached the dinghy and quickly hauled himself inside. He started the engine first time and we were on our way to his friend who was white with panic. We rescued him and his cramps stopped. He said he had nearly drowned so it was lucky we came when we did.

Tobago Cays was the best snorkelling we had seen so far. The coral was so colourful and it was full of life with tiny and large fish so it was definitely a place we would return to.

2nd Feb 1997

We decided to head back to Canouan today (the island where our mooring broke). We still wanted to show my dad's friend the walk to the other side. This time we walked a bit further and came across the local town. The roadside was dotted with tiny little rum bars with locals playing dominoes rather loudly. Instead of gently placing the dominoes down on their turn, they slammed them down so loudly that the table and rum shack shook. We got engrossed in watching the locals play and Dad and Dave joined in. As the evening went on, the music got louder and one by one the local bars competed with each other playing very loud music on the street. It was the weekend and the locals gathered to have their weekly jump up party.

The rum bar we were in was run by a lovely local lady, although us children were a little scared of her at first as she had a bit of a beard. The evening was going rather well at first and the owner kept handing out rum and coke in plastic cups. But then she started bringing out shots of white rum for my dad and Dave. This was the strongest rum you could get. Dad said it tasted like fuel and it was so strong they had to add water to it.

They didn't remember much after that and had rather sore heads the next day. I clearly remember what time we got back to the boat, it was 1am, rather late for us kids!

5th Feb 1997

We headed north to Saint Lucia again as we thought that this might be the best place to leave the boat while we returned to the UK. On the trip up we caught our first Wahoo fish. The girls were so pleased as this was their first fish and it was bigger than Corrie. One night we moored in Jalousie Bay, (the one between the Pitons with the abandoned hotel). This time Dad got talking with Lord Glenconner himself at the restaurant and he spent half a day taking us around plots of land that he was selling in the area. The plots were so overgrown with large trees that it was hard to imagine what view you would get. They were also very expensive so Dad decided to leave it.

That evening we were told by some of the local fisherman that a weather system was passing over so as an extra precaution we attached our stern lines to some palm trees ashore. Wind speeds reached over 40 knots that night and Dad was up for most of the night checking that the boat was okay. Because we were in a marine park in Jalousie Bay we were not allowed to anchor so instead we had to attach ourselves to a mooring buoy. Given what had happened a few days before, we didn't have so much faith in them holding.

We spent the next few days slowly moving up the west coast of Saint Lucia visiting all of our favourite places again before heading into Rodney Bay marina (Where we had finished Arc).

On passing through Marigot Bay, we got talking to an expat at one of the bars there who was looking for a young family to take the part of extras in a German sitcom. We girls jumped at the chance, especially after being told that we would get paid to do it and would be provided with lunch.

On the day of the filming we were told to walk up and down the beachfront acting as natural as possible while the real actors did their parts. It was all rather exciting at first but it soon got boring when we were still walking up and down several hours later. All we wanted to do was play and swim in the beautiful blue waters of Marigot Bay. During the first lunch break we wandered over to the buffet food on display and started helping ourselves to the food. We were quickly told by one of the staff that it was for the actors and not for the extras….ooops. We decided to go and play on the beach. We found a swing over the water's edge so we started taking turns swinging out and holding on for dear life so we wouldn't fall in the water. When it was my turn I accidently slipped and let go and got soaked head to toe, hair and all. On returning back to the film set the director was less than impressed and I was told that I could no longer be an extra due to my soaking wet clothes. Luckily he still paid us at the end of the day so we had a little spending money to buy some local jewellery and t-shirts.

On returning to Rodney Bay, Dave left the boat and flew back to the UK so we were back to being a family of five again. I was rather happy to get my cabin back as I had temporally moved in with Dani and Corrie while Dave took my bunks. When you're stuck in the same bed as your two youngster sisters for a few weeks you start to get on each other's nerves.

By chance it happened to be carnival in Saint Lucia so we headed into town to check it out. It was great fun watching all of the people go by dressed up in their costumes. There must have been at least 500 people taking part and around 10 trucks with huge speakers playing the loudest music you have ever heard. Every time a truck passed we had to put our fingers in our ears, it was painfully loud. I guess the locals must have been used to it or maybe they were partially deaf.

We hadn't really done much schoolwork over the past few weeks, or any maintenance on the boat so we spent the next week catching up on schoolwork and getting ahead on boat chores. We had lots to do on the boat to prepare it to be left in the marina for six months. We gave the boat a spring clean inside, cleaned and polished all of the white work on deck and cleaned all the stainless steel and chrome work inside and outside. This consisted of cleaning and polishing off every bit of rust on the stainless on the boat with a toothbrush and cloth. There sure was a lot of it as most moving parts were stainless.

As we were also leaving the boat in the water over the hurricane season Dad didn't want it to be too near the dock. He got a good rate on two berths so we positioned Rainbow Spirit right in the middle away from both sides. We doubled up our mooring lines and added chains as well. This also gave us the added security of knowing that it wouldn't be stolen or borrowed while we were away for such a long period. The boat was moored so far from the side of the docks that we had to use a dinghy to reach it.

Rest of 1997

Later in the year we returned to the boat briefly and sailed her down to Trinidad where we put her on the hard (dry land). She had been in the water for quite a while now so it was time to give the bottom a good clean and re-paint, before returning back home to the UK again.

Chapter 4
Caribbean Cruising

11th Jan 1998

We arrived into Trinidad from the UK on a very late flight. As soon as we got off the plane you could feel the humidity and heat hit you. The island was so busy compared to the other Caribbean islands. There were more people, more traffic, larger shops, even shopping malls.

By the time the taxi had taken us to Peaks Marina in the port of Chaguaramas it was around 11pm so we were all feeling very tired and grumpy. Luckily Dad had booked us into the local marina hotel that night so we didn't have to sleep on the boat on the hard.

12th Jan 1998

We were up early to check on the boat and see what condition she was in. It was absolutely filthy. So much brown dust covered the decks, rigging and fittings but nothing was damaged or stolen so Dad was happy.

It took a while to locate a long ladder to reach the back of the boat which was a good three metres up from the ground, so there was no way we would have got up without a ladder. The boat smelt musty and damp from being closed up for months but luckily no damage was done to the inside upholstery. Sometimes in such humid conditions the upholstery on the inside can become damp and build up a layer of mildew over it. Decks also occasionally leaked but there was no sign of water damage anywhere.

That day Mum and Dad decided to tackle the boat themselves in the scorching heat and humidity. Much to our relief we were told to get on with schoolwork instead, inside the cool, air-conditioned room of the hotel.

13th Jan 1998

The next few weeks were spent either doing schoolwork or boat cleaning. Quite a few of the navigation instruments onboard were broken so we had a few maintenance companies onboard trying to fix them. When an electrical device is not used for months on end in this salt environment, the electrics can easily corrode causing problems. Trinidad was by far the cheapest Caribbean island we had sailed to so far and the most modernised so it was the best place to sort these problems out and buy new equipment if needed.

The marina was fairly large and we soon came across other youngsters on the hard too, some the same age as us. There were English, Germans, Australians, Venezuelans and some local children. As soon as we had finished work for the day we rushed over to the local meeting point under a big mango tree. We became really good friends with these youngsters and really didn't want to leave.

We also came across a stray dog that lived in the boat yard. Her name was Queen and she had just had a litter of eight puppies so we spent a lot of our lunch breaks with the puppies, giving them food and cuddles.

Word must have got out about the litter because each day we returned to Queen, some of her puppies had been taken to new homes.

5th Feb 1998

It was launch day for our boat. We were booked in for the 11am slot so Dad got us up at 6.30am to prepare. By 11am we were still waiting and found out we were now booked in for 2pm. But when 2pm came they were still running late so by the time we got into the water it was past 5pm. We were in the Caribbean after all and working on Caribbean time. We anchored just off the marina and it was quite strange to be back on the water, moving again.

We were rather tired that evening so had a simple dinner of eggs on toast before heading to bed at 8.30pm.

The next morning we spotted a few problems with the boat. The batteries weren't charging for some reason and there was also a small problem with the engine so the mechanics came back onboard to put it right.

Dad was keen to get back up the islands again so as soon as they were done we motored around to the next bay to anchor for a few hours, before setting off in the evening to do an overnight sail to Grenada. This was a pretty long 18-hour sail and the weather was fairly choppy. Dani and I took it in turns to sit with Mum and Dad on watch. It wasn't the same as the watches on the Atlantic. There seemed to be so many wind direction changes through the night and lots of yachts, tankers and fishing vessels to watch out for. You really couldn't sit down, chill out and just sail. We were constantly on our toes avoiding ships, adjusting sails and changing course to the next waypoint. We did catch two fish en-route, which was good. They were both barracuda, which we had never caught before. We did lose the first one, but managed to get the second one onboard and we had it for dinner. It was a nice tasting fish.

8th Feb 1998

A couple of my dad's friends from the UK flew in to join us on the boat for a couple of weeks. We took them to our favourite islands in the Grenadines including Salt Whistle Bay on the Island of Mayreau and Tobago Cays for some snorkelling.

After anchoring in the cays, we put the dinghy in the water and started to motor to one of the little snorkelling mooring buoys. But on the way our outboard engine cut out on the dinghy. Dad tried to start it, but had no luck. A man from a nearby yacht saw us adrift and shouted to us asking if we wanted a tow. We declined the kind offer and instead rowed back to the boat for Dad to investigate what was wrong with the engine. After stripping the engine apart, finding nothing wrong with it and putting it back together it started first time. We made a second attempt at getting to one of the moorings again. Just as we were passing the same yacht as before, the engine cut out…again. Again he offered to tow us, but Dad insisted we were fine. While Dad tried to start the engine we got the oars out to start rowing, so not to drift down wind too far. After about five minutes of checking various things he gave up and the yachtie and his wife kindly towed us to the snorkelling buoys where we spent rest of the day.

This time we saw some different fish including some beautiful looking squid, box fish, trumpet, angel, butterfly fish and some snapper. The coral seemed to be even more colourful and alive than last time we were here.

19th Feb 1998

Well you know that rum bar that Dad visited with his friend a few months back, the one where they played dominoes and drank very strong white rum, well Dad wanted to take his friends back there again, so we sailed back to the island of Canouan. This time he wanted a grown up night as he called it. Me and my two sisters stayed onboard and watched a movie while the adults went out drinking. At about 1am we were woken by loud footsteps and voices on deck as the adults returned back very merry and noisy.

20th Feb 1998

We were supposed to get up early and take a hike around the island today, but as all the adults were hung over and didn't get out of bed till after lunch, we set off in the afternoon instead. On starting the hike the adults were feeling rather tired so we cut it short and went to a local beach instead on the windward side. It was short lived because Corrie and my dad's friend got stung quite badly swimming. It wasn't until we took a closer inspection of the beach that we noticed lots of baby man o' war jellyfish scattered along the water line.

The last time we took a walk to the other side of the island we came across this big luxury resort being built, called Raffles Resort. We didn't venture too far into it because it was a building site with busy machinery moving around. This time some security huts had been constructed and a lot of the accommodation and chalets had been built. They had even built a reception, restaurant, bar and pool area. It looked pretty fancy and posh so we went to have a nosy and to see if we could buy a drink. But we were turned down. They wouldn't serve us because we were not guests so we left for find a local bar instead.

21st Feb 1998

It was my dad's friends last few days on holiday so we set off early on a six-hour sail to the beautiful island of Bequia. We caught a lovely large big eye tuna on the way up. As soon as we arrived we went straight ashore to take our rubbish to the skips. It had been days since we had managed to offload it somewhere and as it had been stored in the anchor locker at the front of the boat in the heat, it was starting to smell rather bad.

We went to explore Princess Margaret's beach in the afternoon. It was a long beach and it took a good five minutes to walk to the other end where there was a cave. The beach used to be called Tony Gibbons beach, but they had recently changed the name to Princess Margaret's because Princess Margaret has once swam off it.

The left over fish head from the tuna was fairly large and we traded it with a local speed boat so we could get half an hour on their water skis. Who'd of thought that a fish head would be worth anything but the local boat guy was quite happy that he could now cook fish head soup for his dinner. Yuck!!!

That evening we cooked up the freshly caught tuna and had it with some potatoes and veggies, yummy.

22nd Feb 1998

I think we were all finding it a little crowded with the seven of us on a small boat, so we dropped my dad's friends off onshore for the day while we stayed home and had a mini spring-clean. The boat had got in quite a mess over the past week and things had not been put back in their proper places, so it was so much better after we had spent some time cleaning. The decks were salty from the sail up, so we gave that a wash down too. The salt made everything feel very sticky and it attracted moisture so made things feel quite damp.

That evening we booked into a local restaurant called Fernando's Hideaway. It took a while to find because it was up in the hills in the middle of nowhere, so we ended up arriving a bit late. The owner Fernando cooked us a private three-course meal outside on the balcony. His lovely waitress Anna spent some time playing with us and drawing pictures.

23rd Feb 1998

Our guests had now left so we spent the next few weeks catching up on schoolwork again as we really hadn't done much over the past few weeks. There were a few boat jobs that needed dealing with too so Dad tackled those.

The freshwater pump, which pushed water to all of the taps and showers on the boat, had sprung a leak and so was now constantly switching on and off throughout the day, using electricity and leaking our valuable drinking water into the bilge. We only had a short supply of water on the boat and our power came from batteries which the solar panels and engine charged up. When the batteries got low after a few days we had to put the engine on for a few hours to charge them. We didn't have a generator but Dad was thinking about getting some wind generators to help. The fresh water pump was located under the saloon seat which contained all our mooring lines so we had to empty them out just to get to it. Another compartment also had to come out before we were able to get to the pump so it took a while to get to, then Dad accidently broke a part on it while he was trying to fix it. He was rather annoyed because if we couldn't get the spare part ashore then we would be without water for weeks. Luckily a chandlery in the port had one so that was a relief. The fan in the engine room had also stopped working because of a loose cable and one of our fenders had burst so we had to pump up a spare one and neatly sew a new line to it at the top. Luckily Dad was quite good with the needle and thread.

In the evening we decided to have a change and play card games. This allowed us to spend quality time as a family and also conserve electricity because we weren't wasting the power on watching the TV.

27th Feb 1998

There was a huge northerly swell coming into the bay today. The waves on Princess Margaret's beach were so massive that my sisters and I paddled ashore in the kayak and surfed the waves. We had so much fun. It was fairly dangerous as a few times we got thrown out of the kayak and sucked under the water and tossed around in the waves. It was a little like being in a washing machine, but we soon learnt to take it a little easier. You could literally catch a wave in the kayak and it would push you right up the steep slope of the beach before sucking you back out again. Before it dragged the kayak back out we had to quickly jump out and hold it so it didn't get sucked back down the steep beach. The waves were so strong that we were sometimes not quick enough and ended up losing the kayak down the beach.

Mum and Dad remained on the boat, building some new shelving and storage, but as the day went on it got more and more roly, so they shouted for us to come back to the boat so we could move it over to the other side of the bay where it was more sheltered. When we anchor it normally takes one attempt for the anchor to dig in but this time it took us four tries before it caught. We had gotten into the habit of dropping the anchor slowly, nudging the engine into reverse and then when the chosen amount of chain was out we would heavily go into reverse and if it held in about 200 revs (we reckoned this was equivalent to about 45 knots) then we knew it was securely in and we were happy. It was rather amusing to think that when we first started anchoring in the Canaries that we just dropped the anchor and all its chain in one big pile. We had no idea how to really anchor and the boat definitely would have dragged if it had been windy. As I was anchor girl I was in charge of bringing it up and down on an electric winch, controlled by two large white foot buttons on the deck. I also had to make sure that the anchor didn't go down upside down because the nose would have never dug in. The water was so clear and shallow that you could see the anchor on the seabed and on the occasions that it went down upside down we had to start all over again.

So here we were, trying to anchor on the other side of the bay. Every time we dragged, we had to start all over again, taking up all the chain and anchor and then repositioning the boat before putting it all back out again. As we were taking the anchor up we realised that there was all sorts of rubbish stuck to it, bits of plastic, metal and rope. No wonder it wouldn't dig in. The seabed must have been full of rubbish.

That evening we dinghied ashore and phoned my granddad in the UK. We didn't have Internet on the boat or a mobile at this stage so we used an Internet café to ring over the Internet. It was much cheaper than using a pay phone.

Dad decided to treat us to a meal that night so we headed to a waterfront bar called the Harpoon Saloon. But on ordering our food and figuring out how much it was going to cost, mum realised that we didn't have enough money with us so we had to cancel our order and leave. Luckily we counted it before the bill came. It would have been rather embarrassing if we'd all already eaten our meals.

My Round the World Journal

1ˢᵗ March 1998

We had been at anchor for a few weeks now and Dad wanted to give the boat a good charge, so instead of putting the boat in neutral and charging the batteries up that way, we upped anchor and headed out to sea. We fished for four hours with both lines out but ended up catching nothing. I think Dad was getting a little tired of seeing the same sites in Bequia so we made a last minute change of plan and headed into the island of Mustique instead. Mustique was half the size of Bequia and was a private island where some of the world's famous celebs had holiday homes.

The water in the anchorage there was so deep and full of protected corals that we had no choice but to take a mooring for the night. We didn't want to pay a local water boy to takes our lines and attach it to the buoy. Instead we put the dinghy in the water and did it ourselves. Dani and I hopped in the dinghy and took the line off Mum above on deck as Dad steered the boat near the mooring.

We had heard that the snorkelling was rather good so we went ashore to check it out. On the way back in the dinghy, Corrie accidentally dropped her snorkelling goggles in the water. It was around eight metres deep so a little too deep to swim down to get them. They were her only pair of goggles so she was desperate to get them back. There were no locals around to swim down so she offered the first person to get them $5ec (around USD $1.5). I really wanted the money and it wasn't long before I came up with the idea of using the small dinghy anchor on a long line to hook the goggles up on the bottom. This worked a treat and I was able to retrieve the goggles for her.

That evening we went ashore to check out the well-known Basil's Bar. The bar was known for two things, its very high prices and its occasional celebrity spotting. This time we didn't see anyone famous. We found out from the bar that the moorings weren't free so the next day we set off early so we wouldn't get charged.

2nd March 1998

We set off super early for Bequia again, fishing on the way with two lines, but again we caught nothing. Dad was convinced that it was his lures letting him down so as soon as we dropped anchor Dad and I dinghied ashore to find a local chandlery and a bit of food shopping. We came across a well-equipped chandlery called Wallace & Co. As we were browsing the shop we faintly heard Dani's voice on the VHF radio in the background. We thought we had misheard but then she called again. We all had nicknames on the radio - Dad was called Mani from a high school nickname; Mum was called Cinders after Cinderella; I was called Wiggy, also a school nickname; Dani was called Simone, which was her middle name, and Corrie we named Smudge although I have no idea where that one came from. So whenever we called each other up we used our nicknames. So we knew it was Dani as she was calling "Mani, Mani, Mani this is Simone, over." We quickly called her back on the chandlery's VHF but had no reply. We had no idea whether it was serious or not. We still hadn't picked up any food yet so we didn't want to rush back to the boat to find she just wanted a bag of tomatoes. We continued with the shopping, picking up some pizza for a treat, then headed back to the boat. As we neared it we soon spotted, Mum, Dani and Corrie on deck each holding a fender out. A large charter catamaran moored ahead of us was dragging anchor and was slowly drifting close to our boat hitting the side. No one was on board, so we were forced to re-anchor quickly.

The problem with the majority of charter boats was that half of them didn't have much experience sailing and didn't actually know how to anchor. They just dumped it all in a big pile, not digging in the anchor at all, then went ashore. As soon as the wind picked up the chain that was piled on top of itself stretched out, leaving the boat on top of the boat behind them. If the anchor hadn't actually dug in then it would just drag along the bottom and they would slowly drift further downwind, until it finally caught on something, usually someone else's chain along the bottom. The other thing we noticed about charter boats was that as the boat wasn't their own they didn't seem to care if it got knocked about or scratched or hit someone else's boat. Rainbow Spirit was our home and we wanted to look after her so we didn't mess around if she was in danger.

After an eventful morning we got stuck into schoolwork. We had five hours to do a day so if we only did four hours one day, we had some catching up to do the next. Sometimes we even got ahead and could take some extra time off the next day. We must have worked hard because after we finished for the day at around 4pm, Dad took us out on the dinghy for some fun and we took turns being towed behind it. Mum stayed behind and tidied the boat. I think she quite liked the peace and quiet of having the boat to herself, listening to her favourite music on the stereo and pottering about even if it was just cleaning and cooking dinner. We returned to the most delicious vegetable pie.

7th March 1998

We all took a family hike to the other side of the island today. It was a good few hours walking in the heat, but the ice cream Dad bought us at the other end was well worth the effort. That evening we girls headed back early while Mum and Dad took a longer route. For a surprise we made them pasta for dinner so mum had a night off cooking for a change.

Over the past few evenings we had made friends with a local lad ashore who lived on Lower Bay, so in the evening we headed to the beach to play cricket with him. He came over on his little boat a few times to say hi and one night we invited him onboard. This was a mistake as once he was on the boat we couldn't get rid of him. He spilled his drink and food everywhere and was quite disrespectful towards our stuff, treating it as if it was his own. He returned every day and automatically came onboard without even asking. What we didn't know was that apparently as soon as you invited someone into your home in this part of the world they treated like it was theirs, so it was a lesson we had to learn and we had to tell him to not come around again.

8th March 1998

We found a great price on hiring a mini moke in the town centre so we hired one for a few days to explore further inland. Dad soon became interested in plots of land for sale and so we spent a while driving around the different areas and exploring some of the plots there. There seemed to be so many for sale, so much choice. The island was still very unpopulated and unspoilt. We went to view two houses for sale. The first house was only half finished because the owner spent most of the time on their charter yacht. The second house was on a nice large plot with a pretty big pool. They even let us go swimming in it which was rather kind of them.

We explored the turtle sanctuary on the other side of the island and had lunch at the Crescent Bay Hotel, which was located on a beautiful beach on the windward side of the island. On the way back we came across a large bakery run by a local family. It was really cheap and a popular choice amongst the locals. The food was very tasty so we would definitely be coming back here again.

11th March 1998

Our Nan flew into Saint Vincent today. She had flown all the way from the UK and it was the furthest she had ever flown. We sailed to the mainland of Saint Vincent to pick her up. It was a nice gentle three-hour sail. We fished the whole way but caught nothing.

Dad was keen to show Nan Bequia, so it was the first port of call. We took her for a walk around the local markets and she fell in love with a small steel pan so she bought it. We then set sail for Canouan, but unfortunately the weather was pretty rough and Nan became quite seasick. She was sick several times and as there was nowhere to dump rubbish in Canouan, we had to get rid of the sick bags somewhere as we didn't want to store them in the boat. Dad came up with the idea of towing them off the back of the boat so they could get washed out. It worked and at the end of the trip we were left with lovely clean plastic bags.

My Round the World Journal

After Canouan we headed to Salt Whistle Bay in Mayreau where we immediately spotted an English catamaran with two young girls similar ages to us. It wasn't very often we came across children to play with, let alone English kids so we made friends straight away. It was the first time we had been on a catamaran so it was rather exciting. We were amazed at how much space their cat had compared to Rainbow Spirit. It felt more homely somehow with the extra space but then again it was twice the width of our boat with two hulls.

The next day we waved goodbye as both boats headed in different directions. We went onto Tobago Cays and to give Nan a bit of a thrill, Dad paid a local water taxi to take her on a very fast speedboat ride. We held on for our lives it was so fast and Nan loved it.

That evening we motored back to Salt Whistle Bay as it was only next door. While on our way out through the marked channel, Dani appeared from down below with a drink she had made especially for Nan. It had a fancy straw and cocktail umbrella so it looked pretty impressive. She must have been feeling mischievous as she made it with water and washing up liquid. All of us knew what was going on except Nan who took one look at it and said she would have some in a bit. She put it on the floor by her feet and we thought nothing of it. About 10 minutes later she picked up the glass and started gulping it down. We all panicked and grabbed it from her but it was too late. Nan tried to breathe and couldn't. Panic flooded her face while she was gasping for air. We were all running around panicking trying to slap her back and get some water for her to drink. It was pretty scary. We all felt so guilty as we didn't expect her to drink it and stupidly forgot about it. She was finally able to breathe and we explained what had happened. Luckily she just got a bad tummy so it didn't make her too ill. I bet she thought that we were trying to finish her off.

17th March 1998

Dani and I had been collecting used telephone cards for a quite a while and it had become a bit of a hobby of ours. At first we started off with separate collections but soon realised it would be so much better if we put them together and shared the cards. We soon got into the habit of checking around the phones and nearby bins for any used ones. We found more and more and we even put some plastic containers out by the telephone boxes asking people to put any used ones in it. We also had lots of duplicates so were now in a position to trade. We had heard that there was a trader on the next island (Palm Island), which was a private resort. We persuaded Dad to takes us there for a few hours while we went ashore. We found the card trader working behind the bar of the hotel. He was a lovely kind man and he gave us some amazing cards, so many beautiful ones that we didn't have. We couldn't wait to get them back to the boat to add them to our collection. I safely put them in one of the flippers in the dinghy while we quickly swam at the beautiful white sand beach there, before returning to the boat. It was stunning, so perfect and the water was so blue. We headed back to the boat and as usual washed the sand off the snorkels we had. Dad didn't realise the cards were in the flipper and he washed it in sea water next to the dinghy, all the cards came out and immediately sank. There was nothing we could do about it as it was far too deep to swim down and collect them. Dad managed to grab about five but we lost so many more. We were devastated. We didn't even know that phone cards sank, being made from plastic.

That evening we sailed to Union Island and were super happy to see the two girls off the cat that we had made friends with a few days before. We all ate out that night at a well-known buffet restaurant called Lambi's. They even had entertainment, acrobatics, dancers, the limbo and a Rasta guy who walked on glass bottles and balanced on objects. We had a really good time with our new friends so the day wasn't so bad after all.

18th March 1998

It was time for Nan to leave so we took her to the local airport on Union island and waved her off. The plane she was flying on was very small and when we arrived at the airport she was the only passenger so her flight pilot decided to board her early so we quickly said our goodbyes. We stopped at nearly every bar and shop on the way back asking for used telephone cards. The people were very friendly. A lovely lady in the local post office and a guy at the airport gave us some they had lying around. They didn't even want swaps for them.

We returned to the boat and spent the rest of the evening tidying and cleaning. We were all rather tired so had a simple dinner of Alpen cereal.

19th March 1998

Salt Whistle Bay on the island of Mayreau seemed to be a favourite of ours now and as we were only a few hours' sail away, we sailed back there and chilled out for a few days. We took the time to explore the other side of the island again. It was a small island with a steep walk over the hill to the township on the other side. We passed restaurants along the main road and a few guest houses. We came across a donkey who unfortunately had his foot stuck in an old tin can and was hobbling around, but there was nothing we could do about it. We came across a guesthouse called Denis's Hideaway. We got chatting to the owner there who started telling us stories of his life adventures. Three hours later we were still chatting to him, but had to leave as it was getting dark.

On returning to the boat, a change of wind direction had brought a large swell into the bay, nearly bringing Rainbow Spirit onto the beach, so we moved her quickly and re-anchored her further out. One good thing about the swell was that they sent huge rollers up the beach. This was great fun as over the next few days we surfed up them on the kayak and some lilos we had lying around.

Salt Whistle Bay was a fairly small anchorage and it became so full at times that yachts sometimes came into the bay only to find no room so they had to leave. If they didn't get in before early afternoon then there usually weren't any spots left. It was probably the closest we had anchored next to other boats in an anchorage before. Each boat was literally only a few metres from the next in front. When someone picked up anchor behind you, sometimes you even had to motor forwards yourself as their anchor was usually right underneath your boat. On a couple of nights we ended up leaving fenders out dangling next to the hull of the boat in case we moved around in the night and hit another boat.

It wasn't long before we spotted another youngster on a nearby boat. She was about the same age as Corrie, was from Canada and was travelling alone with her parents. They kindly invited us girls onboard for dinner that night.

25th March 1998

We were getting a bit low on supplies and were in desperate need to drop off our rubbish. We headed back to Bequia and just arrived in before the shops closed. We were also getting quite low on fuel and as there were no marinas or docking stations we could fuel up at, we had to order fuel from a fuelling boat. We called them up on the VHF radio and they soon arrived alongside while we were at anchor. This was a smallish sized bright yellow catamaran called Daffodil Marine. They supplied fresh water, fuel, bags of ice, cold drinks and even took your rubbish off you for a small fee. When we were refuelling another charter catamaran decided to moor up next to the fuel boat so our anchor was now holding us and two other boats. It was fairly windy and Dad became concerned that we could possibly drag anchor with the extra weight so we asked them to leave. They didn't want to listen so the fuelling boat ended up untying their lines, which they were not too impressed with.

Mum and Dad were still quite keen on plots of land and properties on Bequia so they hired a mini moke again for a few days to go exploring. We girls were keen to get our schoolwork done so we could play on the beach in the afternoons. Not only was our Canadian friend here and the two girls off the English catamaran, but our other good friends, the four boys from one of the Arc boats were also at anchor, so we spent any afternoon we could playing games on the beach.

Mum and Dad had now found an area of Bequia that they quite liked with a large selection of plots available. An elderly American lady who lived on the island six months of the year owned them. She happened to be on island so we took a drive to see her and ask her about the plots she was selling. We had spent quite a few days looking at different sections and found a couple that we liked. She told us that the first one had already been sold but the second section was still available. Mum and

Dad took some time to decide what they wanted to do.

28th March 1998

We had quite a few squalls go over the boat today so we stayed down below in the dry and got on with schoolwork. We heard a knock on the boat hull. It was a lovely little old man selling some scrimshaw jewellery. He had whale and jackfish teeth which he then hand carved pictures into. He had quite a few double masted boats on the teeth but as Rainbow Spirit was a sloop with only one mast, we asked if he would carve some new ones up. He was happy to do some for us so we settled on a price. He said he would be back in a few days and off he went in his rowing boat. A few minutes later another nasty squall hit and we could see the old man in the distance ahead getting completely soaked and struggling to row against the strong winds. We called him over to take shelter on Rainbow Spirit. He tied off his little boat at the back of our boat and took shelter in our cockpit. We offered him a drink and surprisingly he asked for a nice cup of English tea with three sugars. We didn't normally take sugar in our tea so we girls went on the hunt for some sugar in the kitchen cupboards. We found some and handed a nicely brewed cup of English tea up to Dad and the man on deck. Dani noticed the sugar and while mum wasn't looking quickly snuck some in her tea. Dad sat there drinking his tea saying how nice it was but the man wasn't so sure. He sipped it slowly and asked for some more sugar. We put some more in and sent it back up. He took another sip and asked for some more. Wow this guy really likes his tea sweet. We added some more and handed it back up again. He said "That will do," and sipped it slowly. All of a sudden Dani shot up from her seat, ran to the kitchen and spat out her tea in the sink. "Yuk," she shouted. She said it tasted like salt and after checking the container we realised that we had been using salt not sugar. Oh no, the poor man! No wonder he kept asking for more sugar. By this time he had already drank half his cup, but we quickly whisked it away from him and made him a fresh new cup, this time with sugar not salt. We were actually glad Dani had been naughty and pinched some sugar else we would have never have known.

2nd April 1998

A few days earlier Dani got a splinter in her toe which she tried to get out with tweezers, but ended up digging it in further. Today we noticed her toe had now gone quite septic so we made a trip to the local hospital in Bequia. It was not like a modern hospital back home. This was a Third World hospital more like something from the war. All the beds, machinery and equipment were very old. The nurses took one look Dani's toe and before we knew it they had sat her down, sliced the end of her toe off and stuck a plaster over the end. They didn't even give her any painkillers so you can imagine how upset she was from the pain. Mum took her back to the boat to rest while Dad and I went back up to do some measurements on the section. Dani, however, wasn't doing so well. She was vomiting and her toe and part of her leg had now turned a bright pink so we had to take her back to the hospital. They gave her oral antibiotics but it came straight back up. They told us that she had the beginnings of septicaemia and put her on a drip with antibiotics. She was quite unwell and ended up sleeping in the hospital for two nights. Mum accompanied her. It just showed us how one tiny little splinter or wound in the tropics can quickly get out of hand.

10th April 1998

It was time to head back to Trinidad. Our holiday had come to an end and we needed to haul the boat out of the water and put her on the hard for a few months while we returned to the UK. We cleaned her from top to bottom and we girls were given the task of doing the stainless and chrome work on the boat. After months of being in the water it was coated in a layer of saltwater which had also rusted parts of it. Using a toothbrush we applied chrome cleaner, scrubbed any visible rust and then polished it off with a cloth to leave it super shiny. There's a lot of stainless on a boat so it took us quite a few days to complete this task.

Trinidad was so cheap to eat out in so every evening we ended up eating out at a local pool bar. They served this lovely fresh barbecued swordfish. It was so super yummy we always ate the same thing.

Chapter 5
Saying our Farewells

26th August 1998

After spending a few months in the UK, putting our house up for rent, putting all our furniture and belongings in storage and saying our farewells to our family and friends, we flew back to the boat in Trinidad to set sail on our Round the World adventure.

When we arrived in Trinidad the heat hit us hard. The boat was still out of the water on dry dock and there was no breeze at all so it was very hot indeed, stuffy and full of mosquitoes. We had no mozzie nets to put up so if we wanted the windows open at night, then we also welcomed the mozzies in. After a few restless nights, Dad decided to rent an air conditioning unit. Wow what a difference it made. It turned the unbearable heat into heaven.

Since our last trip, Dad had bought a new outboard motor for the dinghy. We had only ever had a small 3.3 horsepower engine before which was rather slow so we wanted something a little faster and as a backup in case the smaller one broke down. He had purchased a 10hp four stroke Honda. It was so heavy for the dinghy that it weighed it down too much so we had to ask the shop to change it for an 8hp one instead. We were suddenly able to plane in the dinghy for the first time ever. Planing was when the dinghy goes so fast that it lifts out of the water, almost like a hover craft, allowing it to go even faster. It was like being in a little speedboat, except the engine was super quiet because it was a four stroke. We loved it so much we kept taking it out for little trips just to try it out.

It was also Dani's birthday this week so we took the day off to do more fun things. We looked into going to see the turtles but realised that it was the wrong season, so instead we chilled and played games on the boat and had chocolate birthday cake.

Dad had got a new computer up and running on the boat with a nice modern flat screen which he stored in one of the saloon cupboards. He designed and printed out a birthday message for Dani and stuck it to the front of the boat so everyone could see.

3rd September 1998

We were really happy to see that some of our friends from our previous trips were in the boat yard. The Australian and Venezuelan girl told us about a shopping mall not far from the boat yard, so today we went to check it out. We had to catch a maxi taxi, which was a local 12-seater minibus with blasting loud speakers. You could normally hear them coming from a mile away due to the base on their speakers. Each one was customised by the owners and they all had names. They were usually painted in bright colours or funky graphics. They had the flashiest wheels on them and their interiors were normally plastered with Bob Marley and reggae posters. It was about a 20-minute ride to town and only cost 5 local TT dollars, (less than US$1) and a lot cheaper than a standard taxi cab. The new X-Files movie was showing so we went to see that.

4th September 1998

Dad had ordered a bright yellow 2-seater kayak from the States and it arrived today. It was so exciting unwrapping it and we couldn't wait to try it out. It was heavy so Dad helped us get it into the water. None of us has ever kayaked so were all a bit wary at first. It was rather wobbly and felt like it would topple over any minute, but we soon got used to it and got the hang of using the double sided oars.

16th September 1998

Dad had also bought a couple of foldaway bikes for the boat. They were made of aluminium so they wouldn't rust easily and could fold up quite small so that they could easily be stored down below deck. We used the bikes every day getting around the boat yard, popping to the shops and visiting our friends down the road. As the boat was still out of the water we locked them underneath the boat every night onto the metal framework that was holding the boat up. One morning when we came to use the bikes we noticed both gears on the bikes had been removed. It was obvious it was another yachtie because only yachties bought these foldaway bikes and they would have needed the tools to carefully remove them from the bike itself. We had only had them a few weeks and could no longer use them. You can imagine how angry and upset we all were so we printed out posters and hung them up all over the boat yard. We also kept a very close eye out for other bikes that may have had a new set of gears on them but unfortunately we didn't see any.

There was so much to do before the boat was put back in the water. We had to get the life raft serviced and filled back up with new food as the last lot had been in there a few years and was past its use by date. While the raft was being serviced we were invited to have a look at it. This gave us an idea of how large it actually was and what it would be like to be inside with five people. Even though this one was for six people, it seemed such a squeeze to get all of us in. Hopefully we would never have to try it out for real.

We had lots of electricians and engineers come on the boat to service different electrical instruments and look at the engine. Lots of things were not working after not being used for several months. We wanted to make sure everything was in full working order before we set sail knowing that we might not be able to fix things in future ports.

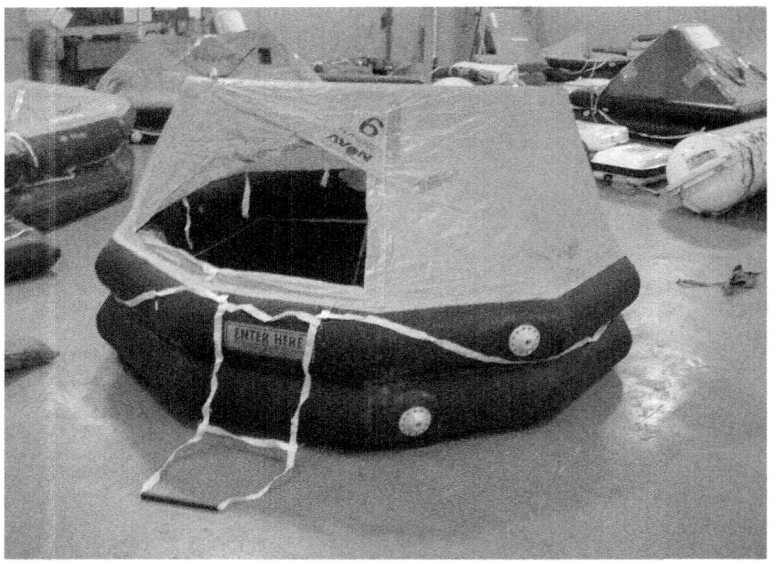

Our Avon six-person life raft in for service

17th *September 1998*

While we were in Trinidad, we had an aluminium gantry built and fixed to the back of the boat that Dad had designed himself. This held two solar panels on top, two wind generators, several hoists for lifting the kayak or outboard out of the water, extra shelving for paddles and fishing nets and there was even room for a towing generator. A towing generator was a propeller attached to a line, which you threw overboard while sailing. It generated a couple of amps which would be enough to run around one light bulb. The gantry would become our little power station and would help to generate free electricity while we were sailing. On a boat you weren't plugged into any mains electricity so we had to rely on a set of large batteries which we normally charged through running the boat engine. This new gantry was going to be like a mini power station.

Trinidad was one of the cheapest Caribbean Islands we had visited, so it was a great place for stocking up the boat with food. Mum, Dad and I took several trips to the local supermarket to stock up on items that we needed for several months ahead. Just to give you a rough idea of how much food that was, we ended up leaving the supermarket with more than 10 large trolleys full of provisions including 100 orange juices, 100 apple juices, 43 boxes of cereal, 100 bottles of pop, 100 tins of tuna, the list went on. We even managed to squeeze some discount from the supermarket for buying so much.

18th September 1998

An American rigging inspector, Billy, came onboard to check over all the rigging today. He ended up taking me up the mast with him and showing me how to inspect the rigging up there and what to look out for. We were each hoisted up in a chair on either side of the mast with the others at the bottom winching us up slowly. I don't think I had ever been this high before. It was rather scary at the very top, especially as the boat was also out of the water, making it even higher from the ground. But I knew that Dad wasn't so keen on heights and in the event that we ever did have a problem with our rigging, I would probably be the most suitable to go up and I was also a lot lighter to lift. Billy gave me good tips on the proper way to climb the mast, what bits of rigging were the most important to check and how to clean off bits of rust. He said the rigging on Rainbow Spirit was in good shape and probably wouldn't need replacing for at least 10 years. That was good to hear.

Now that all the stainless steel on the inside and outside of the boat was sparkling clean, Dani and I tackled the decks. Firstly we cleaned down the wooden teak on them and scrubbed them with an acid like chemical. After six months in the dusty boat yard they were nearly black. We then applied a brightener to bring out the true colours of the wood. What a difference that made, they nearly looked like new. Then it was onto the white fibreglass which covered the rest of the top deck. That needed cleaning then waxing up. Next it was onto the washing and waxing of the hull. It made it so much easier to wax when the boat was out of the water and not bobbing up and down in the waves. We dragged scaffolding around the hull to reach all the parts that we needed to. After we had finished a few days later, the boat was looking like new and it was time to launch her and set sail to Tobago.

24th September 1998

As the sun was going down, we left Chaguaramas Bay in Trinidad and went straight into an overnighter to Tobago. For a change we had a calm and steady sail. We took it in turns to do three-hour watches with me and Mum together and then Dad and Dani. We made such good progress overnight that we ended up getting into Tobago far too early and so the sun ended up being in the wrong position to navigate through the dangerous reefs there. We needed to kill a couple of hours so Dad came up with the idea of practising man overboard drills. While we were sailing along he threw a white fender overboard marking the man overboard, then we quickly practised our man overboard routine. We first had to throw the man overboard pole which floated on top of the water with a long rod on top and flag. This was also attached to an orange life buoy so that went over too. Next we had to run downstairs to the navigation table and press the man overboard button on the GPS. This recorded the exact position we were in so that we had a marker to navigate back to. Then it was back up on the deck to take the sails in before heading back round to pick the fender up. We did this several times and each took turns to navigate the boat back to the fender. We got faster each time and hopefully if it ever happened in real life we would now be more prepared.

We arrived in the afternoon and anchored off Pigeon Point. The beach was stunning with its white sand and crystal clean blue waters. It made a nice change to Trinidad's beaches, which were black in colour.

25th September 1998

My uncle and aunt were joining us on the boat today. They had already spent a week in Tobago on holiday and were now joining the boat for a few days, while we slowly sailed back up north.

We had heard from some locals ashore that some bad weather was on its way, and as Pigeon Point wasn't particularly sheltered we sailed up the coast to a huge bay called Man O' War. We saw hundreds of dolphins en-route and they stayed swimming off the bow of the boat for quite a while. When we arrived we anchored right in the middle away from any boats and put out nearly all of our chain. We didn't quite have enough. As a general rule you should put out at least three times the amount of chain to the depth of water, so if we were in 5 metres, we put out about 15-20 metres. Today we were in 25 metres, so we needed at least 75-100 metres, but we only had 70 on board. Luckily that night the bad weather never came so we didn't get any high winds at all.

On picking up the anchor the next day, it was a real struggle to lift up. The anchor winch, which consisted of an electric winch fixed on to the deck which pulled the chain up and down, started to struggle when we had about 25 metres of chain left to pull up. Even at 10 metres it would hardly move. We knew the anchor could no longer be on the ground, as we were in 25 metres, so thought it must be something attached to the anchor. We were wondering if it was an old shipwreck or something. The water was so deep that it was very dark in colour and you couldn't see more that about 5 metres down. We got to 5 metres, this time the winch would hardly move, so we helped a little ourselves by adding a winch handle and winching too. It got to about 4 metres and we caught a glimpse of the problem, it was a very thick electrical line attached to the anchor, we must have picked it up from the bottom. On looking on the paper chart below, we noticed that there were cables running from the one side of the bay to the other, so we must have picked one up. As soon as it was just below the water surface, we looped a mooring line under it and attached both ends to the boat. The anchor could finally be released and with one quick release of the line, the cable made a fast splash back into the water and we were finally free. It was kind of eerie as we thought we could be bringing up an old wreck or something from the bottom of the bay, so were relieved when we discovered it was only a cable.

We spent a couple of days hopping along small anchorages on the west coast of Tobago, and one day unfortunately noticed that the navigation instruments weren't working properly. The autopilot had decided to pack up so we had to do a quick overnighter and hand steer the boat all the way back to Trinidad to get it repaired. We needed a new autopilot. The old one was only a couple of years old but I think with the boat being left on the hard for a while that the electronics inside it had corroded. Dad decided it was best to upgrade all the navigation instruments to the latest models, so we got spanking new and modern depth, wind and speed control panels along with a new autopilot. The autopilot ran off the GPS and took full control of the helm and direction the boat steered in. This allowed us to set a waypoint ahead on the chart, put the autopilot on auto and then sit back while the boat took over and steered itself. At any time we could turn it off and take the helm, like if we saw a fishing boat or lobster pot ahead and needed to change course suddenly to miss it.

As soon as we pulled into Trinidad again, we girls visited the stray dogs in the boat yard where they were so happy to see us. We fed them and said our goodbyes. They didn't have owners as such but all the yachties in the yard took turns to feed them. Unfortunately none of the females had been neutered so they were multiplying every few months. People tried to give the puppies away as soon as they were old enough, but as soon as they had gone to new homes another female had a litter so it was an ongoing problem. The number of dogs had also grown into a small pack, so in the evenings there had been a few instances where the pack had started to follow yachties back to their boats and were starting to become intimidating to some of them. Luckily we knew all the dogs well enough for it not to be a problem for us. A few of the yachties demanded that the yard get rid of them before the problem got worse, but then you had other yachts who were fond of the dogs and wanted them to stay. So it was a problem that probably wasn't going to get resolved any time soon.

2nd October 1998

As soon as the electronics were fitted, we were good to go again. We picked up lots of cases of alcohol from the duty free shop, re-fuelled the boat at the fuel dock and then did another overnighter to Union Island in Saint Vincent and the Grenadines. This time my uncle and aunt, who were keen sailors, did some watches of their own, so we all had less watches to do and got some extra sleep.

Just before we arrived at Union I was sitting in the cockpit when all of a sudden a huge whale shot out of the water and breached in the distance, making a huge splash. It was the first time I had ever seen that happen before and so it was quite amazing.

Of course while we were at Union we had to check out Lambi's Bar and restaurant again where we had an 'all you can eat' buffet for about USD$15 per head full of delicious Caribbean foods, rice, macaroni cheese, potato salads, fish, crab, lobster and the local conch shell meat. We had great entertainment again with fire dancers, acrobatics and Mr. Invincible, the famous rasta man who performed dangerous tricks, such as walking and lying over freshly broken glass, and balancing on one leg of a chair. He had the longest dreadlocks we had ever seen; they were almost on the floor.

The wind picked up quite heavily in the anchorage that night and although a huge reef ahead sheltered us from the waves, we had no shelter at all from the wind. When it reached over 40 knots, we decided to get the second anchor out on deck just in case we started dragging. We were only 20 metres or so from a reef behind us and with no visibility from the heavy rain, we couldn't risk the chance of dragging into it. The visibility was next to nothing ahead and at any moment we thought that any of the boats anchored in front might drag onto us, ripping our anchor out too. We recorded 45knots on the wind instrument that night and the next day it was still so windy that we decided to put the second anchor out so we could all go ashore and explore.

9th October 1998

It was Mum's 40th birthday today and we spent it on Canouan Island. We made a lovely chocolate birthday cake and gave Mum her presents. She got clothes, earrings, shoes, a purse and some beer glasses.

We were keen to get back to Bequia to show our uncle and aunt the new plot of land we had bought, so we took a four-hour sail up to Bequia and had a fancy meal out at the Frangipani Hotel where a live steel pan band was playing.

It was great having our uncle and aunt onboard. We got to try some new meals which they made. One was creamy pasta and the other was a homemade pizza which we had never had before. They treated us girls ashore to some cake and ice cream one day and before they had sat down at the table to join us, we had already eaten it…..ooops. My uncle gave me a few lessons in physics and maths as there was a few things I didn't understand in my course book and I returned the favour by teaching him how to play the recorder, which I think drove everyone a little mad.

11th October 1998

Dad had hired a car for the day today but was feeling unwell so he stayed on the boat with Dani while the rest of us explored the island. We visited the whale museum where we met a 77-year-old whale hunter who had a large collection of whale bones and pieces on display. We spent a few hours driving down the east side of the island exploring the many unspoilt and deserted beaches.

Late afternoon we returned back to the dinghy dock where we were met by Dad and Dani in the dinghy. At the dock we got chatting to some other yachties for about half an hour when suddenly Dad remembered that Dani had left a cake cooking in the oven on the boat. It would have been well cooked already so we immediately rushed back. As soon as we got near to the boat, we could see dark smoke bellowing out from the hatch. Something was on fire and with panic we quickly ran onboard to see where it was coming from. Dad immediately ran down below into the saloon, but could hardly see anything from the thick black smoke. We girls were all in a panic; we thought the boat was going to burn down so started screaming at the top of our voices on the deck for help. Yachties started appearing from all directions to offer assistance. Dad kept low below and noticed that flames were coming from the back of the oven and had now set the curtains above it on fire. He reacted quickly and grabbed a nearby fire extinguisher. It was a powder one and it soon put the flames out but put a layer of white powder over everything. What a mess it made, so we spent the next day cleaning it all up. The cooker was black inside and out and the curtains were ruined. Luckily the oven still worked... just about; else it would have meant another trip down to Trini again to buy a new one. The automatic lighters inside no longer worked so we had to light the gas oven with a match every time we needed to use it now. We were so thankful we had returned when we did, if we had arrived any later the whole boat might have gone up, and being made from fibreglass and wood, it probably would have caught fire quite easily.

When we first arrived this time in Bequia, we had a local taxi boat come round trying to sell us fish from his boat. He had caught so many, including a large shark. We soon got chatting to the owner, an Italian chef called Maurice, who was opening up a new Italian restaurant ashore. He hadn't yet designed his logo or menu and as Dad had a fairly modern computer onboard he ended up printing some ideas off for him there and then. In return Maurice kindly invited us all to eat at his new, soon to open restaurant to sample some of his new dishes and offer him some feedback.

A few days later we visited his restaurant and he cooked us some plates of raw fish, tuna, shark and barracuda, as well as some traditional homemade Italian pizza. It was all so delicious, even the raw fish which had been marinated in tasty sauces.

That evening while we were trying out the lovely food, Maurice caught us a lizard as we told him we had no pets on board. We took it back to the boat and made a house out of a plastic coke bottle, putting small holes in it for ventilation. We tried feeding it veges and fruit but after a few days it hadn't eaten anything and was actually starting to smell a little bit, so we decided it was best to take it ashore and free it in the trees. It was nice having a pet onboard for a bit, even though it was only for a few days.

While we were in Bequia, my aunt came across an abandoned kitten on the street. Being the animal lover she was, she could not leave it and so she dropped it off at Maurice's restaurant and told him he needed a cat to keep away the mice. He fell in love with it and named it Sharky. A few weeks later we returned and he still had the kitten, this time it was much bigger and quite a bit fatter so he must have been feeding it rather well....maybe it was living off Italian Pizza.

18th October 1998

The batteries on the boat desperately needed charging so instead of doing the usual and charging them with the engine, we decided to up anchor and take a six-hour trip to Mayreau and catch our dinner on the way. We had only been going for an hour when we caught a tuna, so we turned around and headed back to Bequia, catching a second even larger tuna on the way back in. We now had two nice tuna to eat.

19th October 1998

This week after doing our schoolwork each morning, we headed up to the plot of land. We walked up each day to save the taxi fare and it was a good 25 minutes up one of the steepest hills I had ever seen. We spent time clearing a pathway to the plot with a machete. The land was very overgrown with large trees and shrubs. You couldn't even see 10 metres in front of you, let alone the view from the plot, but after a few days of clearing we got the first glimpse of the stunning view out over the bay and township.

Mum had become quite ill around this time. She had developed this very itchy blistery rash all over her arms so we went to the local chemist who gave her some antihistamine. Over the next few days we continued to clear the land but mum's rash had now spread to her stomach and neck and her face was swollen so this time we took her to the local hospital. The doctor there explained that it was caused by a local shrub on the island called Brazil which was highly toxic. He showed us what one looked like and we then realised that they were the bushes we had been chopping down on our plot of land. The doctor gave mum an injection and more tablets which helped a little bit. Dad then decided that it was best to get some local guys in to clear the rest of the land instead.

30th October 1998

It was soon time to leave Bequia and set sail up north towards Antigua where we were finally joining up with the Blue Water Round the World Rally that consisted of around 20-30 boats.

From Bequia we headed north to Saint Lucia, making a quick stop in Saint Vincent on the way. We were lucky enough to spot a large group of sperm whales and got within a few metres from them so that was quite exciting.

Throughout the day Corrie had started to develop these sudden stomach cramps that lasted a few seconds before going. They were starting to come more often and more frequent and got so painful for her that every time one came on, she started crying and screaming at the top of her voice. It was starting to a get a little serious and we thought something could be horribly wrong, so we called into Rodney Bay Marina in Saint Lucia where we had finished the Arc. As soon as we had docked up in the marina, mum jumped into a taxi to rush Corrie to a nearby hospital. The doctors wanted to monitor her overnight as they thought it could be appendicitis. After a night in hospital and taking some stool samples and blood tests from her, they explained that it was due to an ear infection that she previously had, which had now spread down to her intestines. They put her on a number of drips throughout the night and day and when she finally got out, they presented mum with an USD$800 hospital bill…..yikes.

We were all relieved that it wasn't appendicitis and all bought her little gifts to cheer her up on her return. We bought her some soft toys, a Barbie doll, a book and a bag of sweets from the local gift shop in the marina.

The next day mum returned back to the hospital, it wasn't for Corrie this time though, it was to treat the blisters on her arms and now legs that had been gradually getting worse every day. They took a blood test to check everything out and it came back fine. They gave her some more antihistamine tablets and told her not to scratch it because it would spread it more. Before now we didn't realise that it could spread if you scratched it, we had assumed the blisters just appeared where the skin had touched the poisonous shrub. The blisters were however highly contagious and wherever they touched the rest of the body, that area got infected too. Mum had been sleeping with her arms next to her tummy and she now had blisters all over that too.

7*th* November 1998

We were so excited this morning, as today our granddad was arriving from England into the local airport. We took a long ride in a local taxi van to meet him off the plane. We then spent the next three weeks cruising up and down the Grenadine islands with him, showing him our favourite spots. We waved him off at the airport in Saint Vincent which was rather sad as this would be the last time we would see him for a few years now, as we were now starting our round the world voyage.

Chapter 6
Joining the Rally

3rd December 1998

It was time to join up with the Blue Water Rally so we did an overnight sail to Jolly Harbour Marina in Antigua. It was Christopher Columbus who originally gave the island its name in 1493.

It was exciting sailing to a new island that we hadn't been to before and even better as when we went shopping ashore, we found out that they sold fresh milk. We could only get UHT long life milk in cartons on the other islands and it wasn't the best tasting milk, so having fresh milk was a real treat for us all, even better than chocolate.

We girls had completed our schoolwork for the term so we were having a few weeks break from it which worked out well because the next few weeks we spent meeting the other rally members, going to seminars, meetings, parties and getting to know everyone. We were going to be travelling with these people for the next couple of years so they would almost become family really. There were a few boats with kids on board, some our age and some a little older, so we spent most of our days playing games, kayaking and exploring with the youngsters. I think the youngest couple were in their early 30's and the oldest member was a man called Ray who was in his 70's. Mum and Dad were the second youngest couple on the rally, but I would say the majority of members were retired and were sailing as couples.

14th December 1998

English Harbour in Antigua was the next port that we sailed to with the other rally boats. It was well known for its protective shelter from bad weather. The marina there was full, so we ended up anchoring in the bay for a few days until some of the boats had cleared out.

When we came to pull our anchor up it would not budge at all. We had got it stuck on a very old storm chain that had been put down years ago for the large boats to anchor to. It was a very heavy and thick chain so it was a nightmare to get unhooked from it. It was too deep to swim down and free it by hand so we motored back and forth for quite a while until the anchor somehow managed to free itself. If we hadn't have been able to free it ourselves we would have had to pay a local diver to dive down and unhook us.

All of the rally boats anchored stern-to off Nelson's Dockyard which was famous for its restored British Colonial naval station that overlooked the dock. We all decorated our boats with flags for Christmas and put our large Blue Water Rally flags up at the bow of the boat. Now it felt like we were a true fleet and we all looked rather pretty together.

We spent Christmas here and the rally organisers hosted a huge champagne party on Christmas Day. Many of the rally boats had their friends and family out staying with them for Christmas so there ended up being more than 300 people at the champagne party. We were happy because many of the boats' guests had brought their children out with them so we made the most of having fun and playing games.

We made a couple of trips into the capital of Saint Johns for Christmas presents and boat supplies. It was a bit more modern than some of the other Caribbean islands so there was more choice of shops to visit which was good. I even managed to pick up a nice pair of Adidas trainers. The only other place I had seen this style was in the UK so I was rather chuffed when I found them.

While we were there, something quite funny happened to Dad. The rally organisers were constantly organising various parties and dinners ashore and on one occasion we were invited to a rather posh buffet style, cocktail party for dinner that had been put on by someone quite important in the local area. We all put on our best clothes and went to join in. It was rather dark inside the venue and one of the dishes was a plate of chicken wings. Now Dad had been munching on these chicken wings for a while but kept finding that there really wasn't much meat on them at all. He thought they were maybe some type of local bird. It didn't take long for mum to point out that he has been eating people's left over bones, which somehow had ended up piled on a plate on the buffet table. It wasn't funny at the time but we couldn't stop laughing about it afterwards.

30th December 1998

We had wanted to leave Antigua for a while now, but the weather was just way too rough to leave so we stayed a bit longer.

The next port of call on the rally was Panama but we didn't have to be there for a few months yet so we had lots of time to go where we wanted.

While on the Blue Water Rally there would be about 22 different ports where the rally organisers would fly out to and support the fleet for a few days or weeks at a time. They helped with customs and immigration, brought out any mail and boat parts and hosted events and meetings at each port of call. It was a way for the boats to stick to a schedule and have a deadline to get to the next place. As these ports of call were months apart, in between those dates we could sail wherever we wanted.

Today we set sail about 7.30am for an overnighter for the French island of Martinique. The weather was still rough, in fact it was so rough that Dani and I couldn't take our own watches so Mum and Dad had to take them with us.

At about 2.00am while sailing down the west coast of Dominica, we had a very near miss with an unmarked boat that had no lights on at all. We quickly started the engine and immediately changed course to miss it. Dad shouted at the top of his voice, "turn your lights on," just in case they had forgotten but nothing happened. We had got so near to them it shook us all up quite a bit and the adrenalin was pumping. We continued sailing though.

Just one hour later we saw a red flare go off a few miles behind us, followed by another one shortly afterwards. We quickly did a 180 in the boat and headed back in the direction of the flare. We did some mayday relays on our radio and when we neared the vessel we soon realised that it was the same unlit boat from an hour earlier. They must have been trying to get our attention before when they nearly collided with us, but instead we just continued on.

The boat was a steel 40-foot French sailing vessel. It had no engine, no VHF radio and no mainsail as its boom was broken. It only had its headsail left and with such strong winds it was having huge difficulty sailing back towards Dominica, which was now in a windward direction to them. It needed towing in so we passed nearby to it and threw a line, which they missed. We then tried to tow a long line at the back of the boat, passing them nearby in the hope that they would pick it up. They managed to get the line onboard and tied it off but somehow they managed to get it wrapped around their rudder and keel, so we were now towing them backwards. This was no good and very unsafe as the sea was quite choppy so we decided to start again. With all the commotion we ended up losing one of our nice torches overboard while we rushed around on deck. We quickly released the mooring line from our end, thinking they would haul it in at their end, but at the same time they ended up releasing the line from their end as well, causing the line to sink. This was a shame as we had bought this lovely long mooring line especially for transiting through the Panama Canal.

On the third attempt they managed to secure another line on their bow and we slowly made our way towards Dominica. It was so rough at first towing them in that we were only able to go a few knots, but as we neared land the seas and wind died down. We arrived in the pitch black at 5.30am. We released the steel boat so that they could safely drop anchor and we did the same. The coastguard boat came alongside to ask us some questions but we were keen not to lose too much time with them as we still wanted to head towards Martinique that night. Martinique was the next island south so as soon as they had finished interviewing us, we upped anchor and set sail. The weather was now even rougher, so rough that Dad made the call on turning around and going back to Dominica to rest out while the bad weather passed over. As soon as we dropped anchor again we crashed on our beds we were all so tired from such a crazy night.

Dani and me, with customs and the French boat in the distance

1st January 1999

It was New Year's Eve today and also Dad's birthday so we had an easy morning, chilling out on the boat, eating freshly made birthday cake and then had a game of Monopoly which Dad won. In the afternoon we went ashore to check out the local town there. We also introduced ourselves to Fitz and Brian, the two local guys whose boat we had towed in. They told us that they were just out for a casual sail when their boom broke and they couldn't get back to the land in such strong winds. We came across another French boat that happened to have kids onboard so we got chatting. All the kids were fluent in French and as we had been studying the language on our correspondence course, we took advantage of practising our limited French with the other children. We all got on so well that we ended up having them back on our boat until the early hours of the morning. Fitz and Brian also joined us, but Fitz had had one too many so ended up crashing the night on our boat instead.

2nd January 1999

After dropping Fitz back to his home ashore this morning, we found a taxi to take us on an island tour. The island was stunning and less spoilt and populated than some of the other Caribbean islands we had visited. It was covered in lush green rainforests and had a large hot water thermal pool that we all went swimming in. This had to be one of the most beautiful and unspoilt islands we had visited so far and we were all amazed by its natural beauty and friendly people.

While stopping off for lunch in one of the small towns on the island we got chatting to a local guy there who needed a lift down island to Martinique. He asked if we could give him a lift as we were sailing there and Dad agreed on a place to meet him ashore before we set off. It wasn't until we got back to the anchorage that the local taxi driver told us that he was a known criminal in the area and would have most likely have wanted to use us to smuggle drugs down island. Of course we never went back to pick him up before we left.

3rd January 1999

We had slowly been using our water up over the past week or so and were getting rather low. We only held around 250 gallons of water in the tanks on the boat, so enough to last us around 7-10 days with daily showers and washing up. We did have some spare containers of water on deck so we emptied them into our water tank. While pouring the last container in, we noticed that the bottom and sides were covered in long green weed and on inspecting the other containers we realised they all had the same. It must have been because they had been sat in the sun for a while. It was too late to do anything as we couldn't empty it back out again so we decided just to use it to shower in instead and avoid drinking it.

Later in the afternoon, we met up with Fitz again who wanted to show us how to fish properly. We set up a fishing rod in our dinghy and motored slowly around the bay trying to catch something. Unfortunately we didn't even get a bite, but it was fun hanging out with him and getting to know him better. That evening we invited both men onboard for tea to say our farewells.

4th January 1999

We set sail for Martinique today. It may have been a few days later than originally planned, but part of us were glad that we had to tow a boat in because we never would have had the chance to visit and appreciate the beautiful island of Dominica.

The weather was still bad and we had a horrible six-hour slog to the Port of Ville De Roseau where we went straight ashore to check into customs. Wow this island was so different to the others with its modern buildings. It was still one of the regions of France so the local currency was French francs and the local language was French. It may have been twice the size of Dominica but the population was six times the amount so the whole island was more built up with bigger more modern shops, even high rise flats and hotels. What a change in scenery.

The next day it was my 14th birthday so I was taken ashore and Dad bought me a huge bag of pick & mix sweets, a Martinique t-shirt with beautiful fish on and a lovely alarm clock for my cabin. Dani stopped behind when we went ashore and when we arrived back to the boat she had made a lovely birthday cake and had put up happy birthday posters and balloons everywhere inside the boat.

11th January 1999

We spent the next week sailing to Bequia. Mum and Dad needed to do a few last minute checks on the land before we left it for a few years. We pulled into Saint Lucia on the way down to get our alternator fixed and caught up on some boat chores. The stainless needed doing again and the Bimini (the awning over the cockpit) and Spray hood needed re-waterproofing with a spray which stopped the rain or seawater leaking through. We unzipped them from the framework they were attached to and soaked them in a big bucket of the special waterproofing fluid before putting them back on again. We then finished off with an oil based spray. Now no water would penetrate the material and leak through.

From Bequia we set sail for Bonaire on a four-day passage. We had a lovely crossing and the weather was so calm that we managed to crack on with lots of schoolwork down below. We saw lots of ships, several schools of dolphins and we even got to sail past some large whales. As we neared land the wind died down completely so we had to motor the last five hours.

We were all down below looking at charts when we heard a loud engine sound coming from outside. We quickly ran up to check it out but could see no ships. It took us a few seconds before realising that it was a plane buzzing us. They were coming really near, swooping down near the boat and then taking back off again. They did it over and over again, getting very near to the top of the mast each time. We soon got the hint that maybe they were trying to call us up on the radio so we turned it on and spoke to them on Channel 16 (the emergency channel). They were the coastguard wanting to check who we were, what we were doing and where we had come from. I guess they got quite a lot of smugglers on boats so were always on the lookout for suspicious activity. As soon as they were happy with our story they let us be and flew off.

Getting buzzed by the coastguard off Bonaire

16th January 1999

Bonaire was another beautiful island and was well known by tourists for its great diving, snorkelling and wind surfing. All the water off Bonaire's coast had been legally protected since 1979 so the waters were crystal clean and blue, along with super white clean beaches. It felt like we were in Spain or some part of Europe as the architecture was quite different here.

We moored in Harbour Village Marina so had access to the dry land. It was nice for us kids to be able to jump off the boat whenever we wished without having to get in the dinghy to go ashore. A few of the rally boats were also in the marina. One of them had two girls onboard who Dani and Corrie played with every day. In the marina we had the added option of being able to have a phone line connected to the boat. This was amazing as it allowed our family back home to call us instead of us having to try to find payphones ashore.

We spent an afternoon snorkelling and saw so many fish. We even got to see some eels and sea snakes which we hadn't seen snorkelling before. Further inland we came across some bright colourful pink flamingos which we thought were quite funny being on such a small island.

20th January 1999

Today we set off on a four-day sail for the San Blas Islands, which were some very tiny remote islands just off Panama that were inhabited by indigenous Kuna tribes people. We had the same watches, two hours on, four hours off. The weather started off quite reasonable, but as the days went by it slowly got rougher and windier.

On day three we had all the sails heavily reefed and it was gusting up to 40 knots. The boat was rocking all over the place as the wind was coming from behind us now and so everyone was beginning to get a little fed up. We even managed to average 9.5 knots an hour throughout the day so were making very fast progress. When we finally arrived in San Blas the seas were so large it made it very difficult to navigate through the islands and their reefs. The guidebooks advised boats to only enter the islands in calm weather due to the shallows in the area. We had nowhere else to go so Dad nervously navigated through the channel as carefully and slowly as he could. The waves were so large though that we ended up surfing down them coming into the bay, holding our breath as we neared the reefs. Luckily we got into the sheltered anchorage without hitting anything.

A couple of other rally boats were already in and anchored so the next day we went exploring some of the islands with them. One of the islands was heavily populated with kids. The islands were only small and remote so as soon as we went ashore in the dinghy the kids swarmed us and followed us everywhere. The children even took our shoes and some old hairbrush that was lying in the bottom of the dinghy which we had pulled up the beach. Many of the houses had several families living in them at once and most had no electricity or running water so it was quite a culture shock to say the least.

The locals wore very colourful traditional clothing and many children nothing at all. We decided to have a clear out of clothes and ended up taking three huge bin liners of clothes ashore. The kids were like vultures and within a few seconds the clothes had been ripped from the bags, there were so many kids and not enough to go around. There were even boys fighting over our dresses. It was a shame that we couldn't give something to everyone but there were so many kids that we would have had to clear out every item of clothing for everyone to have something.

Unfortunately while we were there a few of the yachties had had equipment stolen from the outside of their boat while in the anchorage so we soon set off for another San Blas island.

This one was called El Porvenir and it wasn't until we had dropped anchor and had a near miss with a small plane that we realised we had anchored right in the middle of an air strip, so we quickly had to move before the next plane arrived in. We caught a shark on the way so that night we had shark for dinner which was very yummy.

The children of San Blas

28*th* *January 1999*

Next port of call was Portobelo, another tiny town about 15 miles from the northern entrance of the Panama Canal. We met up with the rest of the rally boats here as we were all going to be travelling through the Panama Canal locks together over the next few weeks.

We stayed here one night before taking a short sail to the flats, the bay just outside the entrance. Over the course of the next few days we made several trips to the local supermarkets to stock up on food and attend meetings by the rally organisers and the canal staff that would help guide us through the transit process. One day after one of the meetings we watched a boat try to leave the marina on low tide. They were stuck on the bottom and unable to move, but instead of waiting for the tide to come back in and lift the boat off the bottom, the captain put it full revs ahead in reverse. The boat hardly moved, but instead it caused a strong current at its bow from the speed of the propeller. All of a sudden the yacht freed itself from the bottom and shot out of its berth and smashed into the boat behind it. The captain panicked and quickly put it back into forward gear causing the boat to shoot forwards and hit more boats on its path. It was starting to do quite a bit of damage but everything was happening so quickly and people looked on in shock and disbelief. A crowd started to appear and I think the captain was keen to get out so after about 20 minutes of pushing its way through the mud below, they finally left rather embarrassed.

Chapter 7

The Panama Canal

30th January 1999

The day had arrived to finally make our way through the 50-mile canal. Each boat had its own pilot. Ours arrived around 10am and one by one all of the 15 rally boats, along with some other solo yachts, approached the entrance of the first lock. As we approached the first lock each boat joined up with two others, forming lines of three. Men were dotted along the top of the lock edges and threw us monkey fists. These were tiny balls of twine attached to thin lightweight lines that the men were holding at the other end. It was the two outside boats job to then connect their own mooring lines to the monkey fists, which were then hauled back up by the men on land. We were one of the outside boats, so I took one of the bowlines while mum was in charge of the stern. The locks were huge - more than 30 metres wide - and as we all piled in the first lock, the very large gates behind slowly closed. As soon as the gate was sealed, water began to gush into our lock from all angles. There was so much power in the water that it moved the boats around, straining the lines. Water swirled and bubbled around the boats. If you had accidentally fallen in, you would have been caught up in it and may not have survived, so we were very careful to watch our step while we were running around on deck adjusting the lines. As the water filled up each lock, the boats rose and we pulled in the slack on the lines, keeping the boats central to the locks at all times.

While we were travelling in a southerly direction, we could see huge container and cruise ships in the locks next door, travelling in the opposite direction. We went through a total of three locks on the Atlantic side of the canal, which lifted us 26m above sea level. It was such an exciting day, but it went so quickly. Before we knew it we had completed the first half of the canal and it was time to anchor up for the night in the lakes on top. There was no wind that night, so we moored up next to another boat and played games. There were so many mozzies around due to the lack of wind that we had quite a sleepless night itching.

Entering one of the locks of the Panama Canal

30*th* January 1999

As soon as our pilot arrived onboard, we made our way to the Miraflores locks on the Southern Pacific side. This part consisted of four locks which took us back down to sea level. The middle boat had spare crew so they jumped ship to ours and gave us a hand with our lines. This allowed me time to take photos and do some recording on the camera.

We arrived in Balboa late that evening after another exciting day in the locks. We had to take a mooring buoy and for some reason we were not allowed to use our own dinghies to go ashore. I think this was due to being very close to a busy shipping lane. Instead there was a free water taxi which you had to flag down to be picked up and dropped off ashore. The problem was there was only a couple of these taxi boats servicing the area, so sometimes it could take 20 minutes before they saw you waving. That evening we all went ashore and celebrated with pizza at TGI Fridays. In the middle of our table was a collection of helium balloons, which of course didn't last long with everyone on our table sucking in the air and talking chipmunk to each other.

We ended up spending nearly a month moored here because our SSB radio had broken down again and we were getting a new one shipped into the local Balboa Yacht Club. We wanted a working radio to cross the Pacific Ocean with so it took a few weeks to come in. The day it arrived at the Yacht Club we were unable to pick it up as we were shopping in town instead. We decided to pick it up the following day when we were next ashore.

That night we were all asleep when I was woken by a bright orange light through my hatch. I slept on the top bunk and had two small hatches directly above me. The sky was bright orange all around but I couldn't clearly see what was going on. I jumped down and went into the saloon to take a better look through the large windows in there. The Balboa Yacht Club was on fire. It was quite a large building and was totally up in flames. I immediately woke Dad up, who remembered that the SSB radio was inside. He was gutted because it meant that we now had to wait several more weeks for another radio to be shipped in.

We took lot of photos that night while it burnt down and it was still in flames the next morning. On one side of the Yacht Club a yacht had been hauled out of the water to have some work done on it. It was seriously damaged, probably even a right off. Its sails and sail cover had gone up in flames and its fibreglass hull was badly melted.

For a few days Mum and Dad tried to chase the yacht club manager down to see if they could get any money for the SSB but he was nowhere to be found. We spent the next month keeping ourselves busy with jobs, getting ahead with schoolwork, giving the boat a spring clean inside and out and making trips into Panama City to go shopping and exploring.

Quite a few of the nearby yachts had found out that Dad had taken pictures of the yacht club fire. He created a poster with a before picture, a few photos of it on fire and then the after photo of the building in ashes. He was able to sell quite a few copies of the poster to locals and yachts and as soon as word got out, we were having knocks on the hull all times of day from people trying to get their hands on a printed copy.

There were so many seagulls around and one day when we had some left over bread, Corrie went onto the deck to feed the seagulls. She tossed the bread into the air and the seagulls swooped down to collect it. We kept noticing feathers in the water behind the boat and what looked like dead seagulls too. How bizarre we all thought and wondered what had happened to them. Corrie continued throwing the bread from the side and all of a sudden we realised where the feathers were coming from. The seagulls were swooping down to grab the bread and getting sucked into the wind generators at the back of the boat. The blades were spinning so fast that you couldn't really see them, nor could the seagulls. By the time we realised what was happening, we were surrounded by a flock of seagulls and one by one they were getting dragged into the generator and thrown out the other end in pieces. Dad immediately turned the generators off at the trip switch down below so that no more were injured. Corrie felt so bad and was quite upset for the rest of the day.

Panama City was known as a shoppers' paradise with lots of shopping areas and large malls. The clothes were so cheap that you could pick a nice pair of jeans up for only a few USD$ so we all went a bit mad buying clothes. The larger outlet shops were sometimes overwhelming though. I think the staff must have worked for commissions because each store seemed to have about 10 staff patiently waiting for a customer to walk through the doors. As soon as you entered a shop they rushed to help you with your purchases. It was impossible to slowly browse the aisles without having about five people following you closely behind.

As well as the very busy and modern side of town there was also the old side of town, which was a bit of an historic attraction with its cobblestone streets and very traditional Spanish looking houses. The buses were so bright and colourful, in fact the whole city was very colourful. Even the slums had very brightly coloured buildings. We loved the hustle and bustle of this super cheap and colourful city.

When the second SSB radio finally arrived Dad couldn't get it to work. We had some yachties come onboard to take a look but they couldn't get it to work either, so we had to take it ashore to a local service agent to get it fixed.

Our fresh food supply from Panama

27th February 1999

After being on the mooring in Balboa for nearly a month we finally set sail for the Galapagos Islands.

The rally boats had left weeks before us and were already in their next port of call at Ecuador. We had to give Ecuador a miss as we had run out of time and so headed straight for Galapagos.

We had a lovely six-day sail into Galapagos. En route we saw lots of large ships, dolphins, whales, even some sharks. We kept coming across very strange brown patches of water. We had no idea what it was but Dad thought maybe it was due to some volcanic activity underneath the water as when we neared them, the water temperature seemed to go up. At first we decided to avoid them and manoeuvre around them, but they were all over the place so in the end we decided to just sail through them. We never did find out what they were.

On the fourth day we lost all wind so had to take in all the sails and switch on the motor. We kept seeing twisters in the distance, which we guessed must have been water spouts from the ocean. The weather was so calm that we decided to pump up the dinghy so we could travel alongside the boat and take some photos of us sailing. We had many photos of other boats sailing past but never of Rainbow Spirit so we thought this would be the perfect opportunity, especially with the lovely clear blue skies and blue oceans behind. As soon as we were about to put the dinghy in the water, the wind picked back up, so we had missed the lull.

As it was so calm, Dad decided to share watches instead and put Dani and I together to share a watch. This made it a lot easier than doing it by yourself, but Dani kept falling asleep so I had to keep nudging her to wake up. It seemed pointless for both of us to stay awake, so we took it in turns, 20 mins on while the other had a nap, then we swapped over giving the other person a nap.

We did catch a couple of fish en route, a new species that we had never caught before called a bonito. Luckily we had some plastic fish guides listing all of the Atlantic and Pacific fish on them, so every time we caught something new that we didn't recognise, we could see exactly what it was from the card and check that it was safe to eat.

Chapter 8

Stunning Galapagos

5*th* March 1999

We arrived in Galapagos in the early afternoon. We were one of the last rally boats to arrive and many of the boats came over to greet us in their dinghies when we came in. For some reason we all had to anchor in the same direction as each other, with a stern anchor out. The heavy stern anchor was down below in the saloon, under some screwed down floorboards, under some more screwed down wood which was under a huge heavy pile of spare chain, so that took a while to get out. We then had to get it up on deck very carefully without scratching any varnish work on the interior of the boat.

One of the other yachties took the heavy stern anchor in their dinghy and dropped it away from the back of the boat. I was in charge of tying its line off at the stern and somehow managed to get my arm trapped between the taught line and the boat railing. I started screaming in panic as it squashed my arm against the railing, but luckily one of our friends was there in his dinghy to quickly free me. It made me realise how fast accidents can happen on a boat. Luckily I was only bruised this time but I was left shaken for an hour or so. Mum gave me some sugar water to help me feel better, apparently it was supposed to be good for shock, or maybe it was just for comfort.

As soon as we had moored up, one of the rally organisers came over with a boat full of customs officers to check us all in. They were all so smartly dressed that we had photos taken with them which they didn't seem to mind. They did their usual checks inside and outside the boat checking for suspicious substances onboard and checking what meats and certain food items we had brought into the country.

Wow, Galapagos was so different. As the islands were volcanic their landscape was quite dry and barren. The climate was so much hotter here being on the Equator and what a difference it made just being that slightly bit further south. The local town there was very smart and tidy and the streets were dotted along with tiny bars and restaurants.

That evening we went out for a meal with some of the other yachties who we hadn't seen for well over a month. After the meal we all headed to a bar. One of the youngsters from the rally, who was around 17, ordered a cocktail from the bar and the barmaid said she would bring it over to our table. When she returned she walked over to him, lifted his shirt up, poured salt and lemon on his stomach, licked it off, and then kissed him. Wow, we were all in shock. The men joked that they wanted to order the same drink as the lad did. The bar lady was around 40 and we nick named her granny Barbie.

From there we went onto a local dance club with some of the other rally members and youngsters and all stayed out till 4.30 in the morning. We had so much fun dancing that none of us wanted to go home.

The Galapagos Islands were famous for their vast number of native species and were studied by Charles Darwin in the 1800s. It was here that he was able to help prove his theory of evolution by natural selection in which certain species over time adapted, mutated and developed certain characteristics and behaviour to survive better in their surroundings. As each island was quite a bit different he found that the species on one island had different characteristics to the same species on one of the other islands. Over time the species had naturally adapted to their surroundings to survive better - a theory well known today as evolution.

The 16 different Galapagos Islands and their surrounding waters were part of a highly protected national park and biological marine reserve. This meant that many of the islands could not be visited by yachts unless they had a special permit and guide accompanying them. It was easier to leave Rainbow Spirit anchored off the main island of Santa Cruz while we took a small cruise ship around the other islands that were not inhabited by humans, only wildlife.

Dad booked up a cruise for a week. It was rather exciting for us girls packing our small suitcases to go on a much larger boat. The ship seemed pretty normal on the outside but the inside was amazing, as it had just had a re-fit, so everything was brand spanking new. We arrived with two other couples from other rally boats so it was good to have familiar faces for company. We actually arrived on the cruise ship about three hours earlier than all of the other guests and the rooms weren't quite ready so some of the staff onboard decided to take us on a little dinghy adventure to an area called The Turtle Cove. We saw so much wildlife; the waters seemed to be overflowing with it. We saw turtles, sting rays, sharks, starfish, large frigate birds and blue footed boobies which were local birds that were named after their bright blue feet.

When we arrived back onboard we got to check out our lovely cabins before sitting down to a beautiful all-inclusive buffet lunch in the boat's large restaurant. The food was some of the nicest we had tasted and we felt truly spoilt. It wasn't long before we had landed on the next island. We were introduced to our group and guide and were dinghied to the shoreline. As soon as we stepped ashore we were overwhelmed at how much life there was with so many sea lions, iguanas, gulls and bird life. They seemed to have no fear of humans at all, probably because we had never been a threat to them. This was great because it meant that you could get super close.

We spent the next few days doing activities throughout the islands. The beaches had the most purist white sand and were dotted with happy bathing sea lions. We went swimming with penguins, sea lions and even schools of at least 15 large hammerhead sharks which were bigger than Dad. We swam with smaller whitetip sharks, which were rather scary, but our tour guide assured us that we were totally safe as they weren't interested in humans. The dinghy was always nearby if ever we wanted to get out of the water. We spotted sea snakes and octopuses. Every day we encountered new amazing creatures.

Posing with the local sea lions in Galapagos

We had seen lots of dolphins on Rainbow Spirit before now, but on one particular day we went by dinghy along one of the rocky coastlines to check out the dolphins and we were totally blown away. We came across schools of hundreds of them and motored along with them for more than 20 minutes. They surrounded the dinghy and swam so close to the bow that we could reach out and touch them. We had never seen so many in one place; it was rather overwhelming but yet a truly amazing experience.

On one of the islands there were so many land iguanas that you literally had to watch every step so not to tread on them. There were thousands of them bathing on the dry volcanic rocks. Many of them were dead and dried out due to the effects of the El Niño a few years before. The El Niño caused a change in water temperature around the islands so certain foods such as algae, which the iguanas fed off, diminished. This unfortunately resulted in thousands of deaths to the marine iguanas, birdlife, the fur seals and the sea lions.

On another island we were watching some female sea lions on the beach when our tour guide Fabio decided that it would be fun to take a closer look with Corrie and Dani. They bent down and crawled along the sand slowly, taking their time getting nearer and nearer to the relaxed and sleeping sea lions. Some were aware what was going on but they didn't mind at all. When they got within about half a metre all of a sudden a large male came running over making a roaring noise at the top of his voice. He was not so happy that his women were being disturbed. Dani got up and ran back to us and Corrie tried to do the same, but Fabio told Corrie to remain very still and continue lying down with her head in her hands. The male seal lion took a few minutes to smell them, before deciding that they weren't a threat and then let them be. It was rather nerve wrecking because the sheer size of him would have squashed both of them, but luckily the guide was there to keep us all calm.

Corrie and our tour guide getting up close

One island had the world's largest land tortoises that were unbelievably massive. Some were more than six feet long and over 160 years old.

Another island was inundated with bird life. There were red and blue-footed boobies, hawks, frigates, finches, mockingbirds, albatross, cormorants and many more. Many of the birds were either nesting or calling for mates so the island was rather noisy indeed.

The cruise soon came to an end and we were so sad to leave. It was one of the best adventures we had been on, so much magical wildlife and such a beautiful boat, they really did make us feel like royalty while on board.

Chapter 9

The Pacific Crossing

16th March 1999

After a morning of stocking the boat up with fresh food supplies from ashore, filling the boat up with fuel and water and doing the last minute safety checks on board we set sail on our three-week trip across the Pacific.

When we came to get the stern anchor up by hand in the dinghy it was impossible to budge as it was so well dug in. We had to connect it to the anchor winch on the front of the boat to help pull it up. Even the electric winch struggled with it so it must have been dug in very well indeed.

As usual we were one of the last remaining rally boats to leave port again. This was probably due to the fact that we were normally late arriving in. The others always seemed to be days and some even weeks ahead of us. We weren't the last boat though, there were a couple of other yachts that seemed to tag along at the back with us. It was on this trip we decided to call our little group 'the back enders club' and kept in touch daily via VHF radio. When we lost VHF signal we reverted to using the SSB instead, which travelled further away. But every time we used the SSB, strange things seemed to happen with the other instruments and the autopilot on board, so it was interfering somehow. I guess the service shop in Panama hadn't fixed it properly as every time Dad used the SSB the autopilot went off, taking the boat off in a random direction, so we had to hand steer instead.

One of the wives on another boat began to read daily stories over the radio. We tuned in at the same time every evening to share our position, talk about the weather and listen to the next part of the story. This particular story was one she had written about a family of blue-footed boobies.

For the first few days there was very little wind, so we ended up motoring quite a bit and our fuel supply was going down quite fast. The seas were so calm that we were able to fill up the boat with spare fuel from plastic jerry cans that had been stored on deck at the back of the boat. The only wind we got was when a nasty squall went over us giving us a little wind and lots of rain. It was good to have fresh water on the decks again as it helped wash the salt water and dead flying fish off.

Some of the other boats didn't have spare fuel so they decided to head a little south to pick up some wind. We had a limited fuel supply and would run out if we had to motor all the way, but we decided to stay on track and after a few more days the wind picked up and we averaged about 6-7 knots. We started fishing and one day caught three fish. The first was a bonito again but we ended up losing it just before we landed it. The second fish was a very small baby dorado, but it was so small that Dad decided to free it and then third time lucky we caught a much bigger dorado which we decided to eat.

At one point we came across a massive whale which came very close to the boat before deciding to circle us. It must have been about 20 foot, about half the size of the boat, so it was a little intimidating being circled by it. I think it must have just been inquisitive because it eventually swam away.

As the wind was mostly behind us and we were downwind sailing with both sails poled out, we were constantly rocking from side to side. There was not quite enough wind to keep the headsail filled and every time the boat rocked back and forth, it flapped, causing a sharp loud bang. Weeks of flapping caused it to develop tears all along the bottom, so one morning Mum and Dad spent their time patching it up. Luckily the ocean was so calm that we didn't take any waves on deck while they were up there.

Every morning Dad went around the decks pulling off squid and flying fish that had landed on it the night before. Some of the other yachties ate them but to be honest we didn't really know what to do with them so we threw them back in the water instead.

The whole crossing was ever so gentle apart from the constant rolling, but it didn't stop us from cracking on with schoolwork. Every evening we tuned into our little 'back-enders club' net to give each other our position and to tell each other short jokes. It became a little like the comedy channel and was a highlight of the day. Nothing seriously went wrong on the trip, just the sail ripping and one of our jib sheets wore through and snapped where it was attached to the headsail. We quickly re-tied it so we had a very easy trip.

About 900 miles from landfall we spotted some birds, one that we recognised as a blue-footed booby from the Galapagos, but he didn't land onboard for a rest.

Samantha Saunders

Chapter 10
French Polynesia

4th April 1999

After 20 days of being at sea, we finally made landfall into Taiohae Bay, on the island of Nuka Hiva, the largest island of the Marquesas. My gosh it looked a little like Jurassic Park from a distance, the land was covered in lush green steep high rise mountains.

The Marquesas Islands consisted of about 10 different volcanic islands that were part of French Polynesia, of which the official languages were French and Tahitian.

We anchored in the large and very beautiful bay in around 20 metres of water. When we got in the dinghy to go ashore we were shocked by the huge amount of weed which had grown on the hull of the boat. The barnacles at the very back must have been about 4 inches long. It's funny how they just appear from nowhere after being at sea for three weeks.

As Nuka Hiva was one of the Blue Water Rally ports of call, one of the organisers was here to welcome the yachts in. They organised a lovely buffet party for all of the boats along with some traditional dancing by the local people and a laying ceremony where they placed wreaths of flowers over the boat owner's heads.

We came across an American yacht in the anchorage not too far away and became friends with their son who was the same age as me. One of the rally boats that had the two young girls onboard was also in so we spent time playing together and going off on adventures exploring in the kayak.

Coming in goose winged to Nuka Hiva, Marquesas

We took a tour of the island while we were there and saw lots of beautiful unspoilt bays, a historical sacrificial site and for lunch we joined in a roast pig feast that had been put on by the local community. They had sacrificed a pig and had cooked it below the ground. They then laid a delicious selection of local foods on large palm leaves, scattered on the ground for us to help ourselves.

10th April 1999

After a day or so of catching up on boat chores, cleaning the weed and barnacles off the hull and catching up on all the washing (which took mum a whole day to do as it was all to be hand washed, as there was so much of it), we sailed to the next bay which was an hour away called Hakatea Bay, or better known as Daniel's Bay. It was so well hidden that we actually sailed right past it at first. The mountains here were even more breathtaking and we got to anchor right next to them. The scenery was so amazing that we spent a few hours motoring the boat up and down trying to take photos from the dinghy, with the stunning view in the background.

We took a 4-5 hour hike to the foot of a 350 metre high waterfall, the highest of the many on the islands and one of the world's highest. We crossed over three knee high streams to get there, getting our feet wet each time and on the way back when it was starting to get dark, we got a little lost for over half an hour which freaked us out a bit. Luckily we managed to find the way back to the track before we lost all of the daylight.

Beautiful scenery of the Marquesas

Over the next few days we slowly motored round the coast to some other anchorages. Some were just way too roly due to a large swell coming into them. It was also impossible to get ashore in the dinghy due to the large breaking waves so we had to move a few times.

We kept bumping into another rally boat called Music that had a teenage girl onboard. Her name was Jenny and she was around four years older than me. She was very good at drawing so while all the parents got together she gave us some art and drawing lessons down below in her saloon. I think she started off a little hobby for us because over the course of the rest of the trip we started sketching and painting in our spare time.

14th April 1999

It was time to leave the Marquesas Islands and head to the remote islands of the Tuamotus, some 500 nautical miles away and a good four-day sail.

The Tuamotus Archipelago formed the largest chain of atolls in the world and consisted of around 78 islands and atolls. Some were used for extensive nuclear testing by France between 1966 and 1996 and are now guarded by the French forces. Atolls were actually the rim and craters of sunken volcanoes so we had to carefully navigate around them through marked channels. We were not protected by wind but the atoll edges protected us from the large waves of the Pacific Ocean.

Once we'd navigated and anchored in the first atoll another three rally boats joined us so we all got together that night for a catch up.

Over the next couple of weeks we did a lot of exploring around each atoll. Dani was out on the kayak every day, exploring the many white sandy beaches. The islands were hardly inhabited so there was nothing to do at night except get together with the other yachties over nibbles and drinks and play board games or watch movies.

Each day we moved to a new atoll and instead of navigating the hazardous reefs alone, we went in groups of about four or five boats. We had to time it right so that the tide was slack. If the tide happened to be coming in or out it caused strong currents making it dangerous to navigate the reefs. Many of the atolls only had one or two entrances to choose from and many of them none at all.

One of the atolls was inhabited so we went ashore looking for fresh bread but we were unable to find any. We did get chatting to some boat boys who sold us a load of pearls. More than 10 years later when Dad went to get them made into jewellery for mum for their 30th wedding anniversary, we found out that more than half of the pearls were fake and plastic. We still got a good deal at the time though.

One of the boats had the oldest member of the rally on it. Ray. He was now sailing single handed as his crew had all left. He told us he had never been snorkelling before in his life so one day we took him snorkelling for the first time. He did rather well considering he had never done it before. The fish were great; we saw beautiful parrotfish and the fattest black sea slugs you could imagine. We saw a baby whitetip shark but when Dad spotted a larger one a metre long we decided to call it a day.

There was so much coral around when we anchored that we kept getting our anchor chain stuck around it so Dad was forced to swim down and free it several times. Luckily it wasn't the anchor that got caught otherwise it may have been more of a problem to free.

24th April 1999

Jen and me jumped ship and joined Ray on his boat Lady Rosemary. It was only a two day sail to Papeete (the capital of French Polynesia) in Tahiti, but we thought we'd try something different and offer him a hand with his night watches as he had no crew. Jen and I shared three-hour watches on and off with Ray but when we were supposed to be sleeping, we ended up talking instead, so we didn't get much sleep at all.

One evening when we were both on watch, Ray appeared from down below murmuring something. We couldn't figure out what he was saying as he was hard to understand. We thought maybe he has been drinking and was slurring his words. It was only when we came to get him up for his watch that we realised he had taken his false teeth out causing him to talk funny. And there was us thinking that he was drunk ha ha.

Jen and I cooked all the meals onboard during the trip and I had such a lovely time on Ray's boat. It was exciting to try something new and learn to sail a totally different boat.

Dad was pretty safety conscious on Rainbow Spirit. Even during the day if it was calm he still wanted us to keep our lifejackets on and clip on whenever we left the cockpit to go on deck. We didn't have to on Ray's boat as he was pretty laid back and quite happy for us to go on deck without being clipped on at all. We did make sure that we all clipped on at night though.

26th April 1999

Papeete was quite a bit more built up than we expected. It was a buzzing little town, or maybe that was because we had been so isolated for the past few months that we were pleasantly surprised to moor up to some civilisation. Many of the other rally boats were moored stern-to the dock next to each other. This was another one of the rally stop offs, so one of the rally organisers flew out to welcome the yachts in.

Rainbow Spirit arrived a day later and moored stern-to with the anchor out the front. When another rally boat came in next to us, they ended up ripping out our anchor and sending us crashing into the harbour wall behind. We quickly had to move, but on taking up our anchor, we ended up ripping our neighbour's anchor up, so we were all in a bit of a pickle for a bit. I think all the chains must have been laid over each other. All of us had to re-anchor again and after a couple attempts of dragging, we finally all dug in and were settled again.

That evening we headed to a local food market and ordered some food from the local "roach coaches" which were little vehicles selling all kinds of food. Some of the food was cooked so spicy that we couldn't eat it.

A couple of nights later Dad decided to have a party aboard Rainbow Spirit. I don't think we had ever had so many people on board. The drinks were flowing, music was blasting out the cockpit speakers and people were dancing all over the deck. Random people walking along the dock were invited onboard by people and more and more people piled on. At about 3am everyone finally went home.

Our American friend was also a few boats down and one evening we were invited onboard his boat by his parents, who made us some super yummy homemade pizza. We had never made homemade pizza before and thought it was so much fun rolling out the bases and being able to choose the toppings.

By now we were getting low on fuel so we ended up motoring to Maeva Beach up the coast which had a fuel dock. It was so windy and rough when we got there that we simply couldn't dock up and re-fuel. We were desperate for fuel though, so with help off another rally boat, we borrowed some of their jerry cans and made several trips to and from the fuel dock in the dinghy, slowly filling up the tank. It was a very long and wet process as it was so rough. The dinghy nearly sank with water so I scooped it out as fast as I could. It was cold, miserable and wet but it needed to be done, and afterwards we were relieved that the boat was finally full with fuel again.

3rd May 1999

Our next port of call was the neighbouring island of Moorea, about 15 miles to the west. This island was a lot smaller than Tahiti but was a lot prettier. We followed buoys and leading lights into the very beautiful 20m deep Baie De Cook. The scenery was just stunning.

The next day we took a 10-mile hike with one of the other boats to a viewpoint on the island. On the way we passed a little supermarket so stopped to have some chocolate ice cream before continuing. We had a lovely walk on the main road all the way. We passed pineapple and papaya gardens as well as some old burial sites. I couldn't believe that the pineapples grew in the ground, I always assumed that they grew on trees. Jen's dad John was with us on this walk and one of his flip flops that he was wearing broke so he ended up having to walk barefoot. It wasn't long before we found an abandoned old flip flop at the side of the road, so we grabbed it for him to use. Luckily it happened to be the correct foot, even though it was a little on the small side. But he put it on anyway and we couldn't stop laughing about it.

We dinghied out to a few of the snorkelling sites around Moorea, but the weather was rather rough and we didn't see many fish at all so returned home early.

The next stop was at a neighbouring island called Raiatea, which was a night's sail away and Tahiti's second largest island. We stopped there for a night before heading to the next island, Tahaa, known as Vanilla Island as it produced 70-80 percent of all French Polynesia's vanilla.

11th May 1999

After freeing our anchor chain from a couple of coral heads, we took a six-hour sail to Bora Bora where we navigated through the stunning reefs and caught a mooring buoy.

This had to be the most stunning island yet. The island was surrounded by a large reefed lagoon and in the centre rose two huge extinct volcanic peaks. The view and scenery was breathtaking. The shoreline was dotted with some exclusive resorts and hotel chalets that sat over the water's edge on stilts.

We hired scooters for the day with some friends and spent the day slowly cruising around the island on the mostly tarmac road that followed the perimeter of the island. We all had such a fun day on the scooters that we really didn't want it to end.

The island was so beautiful that we decided to stay a bit longer, before setting sail for Tonga.

Chapter 11

The Worst Storm

17th May 1999

After a trip ashore to stock up on fresh supplies we set off on another long trip towards Tonga. It was around 1600 miles so would normally take about nine or ten days to reach landfall. On this particular trip it was like setting off on the Atlantic Crossing again, with a constant 25 knots and fairly largish seas. From the start of the trip the wind gradually increased and so did the size of the waves.

The weather report showed a nasty storm headed straight for us and so we were in for a bit of a nasty ride ahead. Visibility became so bad due to the heavy rain that someone constantly had to be on deck. The waves got so big and the wind so strong that we were forced to take in all sails and clamber onto deck to put up the bright orange emergency storm jib. We had no choice but to turn in the same direction as the waves to do this. We were shooting down the waves so fast that the boat almost lost control sometimes. We were averaging over 12 knots an hour and the winds were a constant 40 knots. We all put our heavy weather gear on for the first time since England and were forced to dodge ships by using the radar as the visibility was so bad. We all prayed that the bad weather would be over soon as it was starting to become quite dangerous.

On the night of the 23rd we were giving our daily position to the rally net on the VHF when we heard a distant voice interrupting with a mayday call. We girls were speaking loudly in the saloon at the time and Dad suddenly shouted for us to be quiet as he tried to listen in. It was one of the other rally boats and the elderly female skipper and her young 21-year-old crew member were about to climb into their life raft before making a last attempt to do a mayday call. Their boat was sinking and we just managed to get their position before they abandoned the sinking vessel. The storm was so bad you could only imagine what sea conditions they now had to go through in their liferaft. One of the other nearer rally boats changed course and headed straight to them.

A neighbouring island, Niue, sent planes to locate the life raft and set off emergency flares to help the rescue yacht identify it in such heavy seas. I think they were at sea for a good few hours before finally being rescued. The yacht eventually found the life raft with the help of the Niue Coastguard and as the skipper and crew climbed on board, they had no choice but to let the life raft go. It was far too windy for them to get it on deck and far too dangerous with all its long dragging lines.

Everyone was so relieved when we finally heard that they had been safely rescued. They were still unsure on why the boat sank though, they just said they were on watch when they realised that down below had filled up with water and the floorboards were afloat. They tried to keep the boat afloat for as long as possible, pumping out the water, just so they could get the call in on the rally net before abandoning ship. The captain said it was such as shame as she saw her laptop down below but it was too dangerous to go down and get it. The water had become live from the batteries being submerged underneath. The laptop had all her photo's on of her travels from the past two years.

The storm was still getting worse so we decided to pull into Niue. We could not believe how calm it became as soon as we arrived in the shelter of the land. It was quite remarkable what a difference it made and what a relief it was for us all. Everything was so peaceful and calm in the anchorage that it was hard to imagine that is was so rough out at sea. It was a bit surreal for the boat to be still after being is such rough weather for so many days.

It took us a good few days to recover and get the boat back to normal again. It was a total tip after being in such terrible weather for so long.

Dad navigating in rough weather off Niue

The island of Niue was so unspoilt and beautiful. The majority of people spoke English and the currency used was the New Zealand dollar. The tide was so large that every time we went ashore we actually had to haul our dinghy out of the water by crane. The water was some of the clearest we had seen, you could see straight to the bottom, but as there were black and yellow water snakes everywhere, we avoided swimming in it.

We hired some bikes while we were there and spent a day cycling around the island doing a tour. We cycled to the windward side and we could see the huge waves out at sea still. We were glad we were not still out in them.

31st May 1999

The storm had now passed over so we set off again towards Tonga. What a difference a week had made on the weather. This time we had no wind at all and on the odd occasion we did get a slight breeze, it was right on the nose, so we ended up motoring the rest of the way. I guess the storm must have sucked up all the wind in the area, leaving a bit of a calm behind. The sea was completely flat so we had no excuse not to crack on with schoolwork.

We landed in Tonga just two days later and were guided through the entrance reefs to Sunset Anchorage by a guide boat. The rally organisers were there to welcome us in and we had just missed a large briefing by them so were given a one on one by the organiser.

That night we celebrated with all the other rally boats as we had now reached the half way mark of our round the world trip. We had a great buffet dinner put on by the rally and got to see a fantastic Tongan traditional dance.

3rd June 1999

Corrie was 10 today and we sailed to Nuku'alofa, the large island nearby. While Corrie was ashore with Mum and Dad, we made her a lovely birthday cake onboard.

We spent the next few days sailing to some of the smaller islands of Tonga and had many get-togethers and movie nights with some of the other rally boats. We made friends with an American couple who sailed their 60-foot boat by themselves. They showed us around their boat, but to be honest it was more like a home. What a difference an extra 15 feet made, it even had a bath onboard and was carpeted throughout.

Steve, one of the rally members, used to teach computer courses back home so he kindly offered to teach us the basics of computing over the next few weeks. He brought props and everything to our boat to demonstrate what he was talking about. We learnt quite a bit from him and it made a change to doing our normal schoolwork.

I started making a Rainbow Spirit flag for the bow of the boat. Each boat already had a large Blue Water Rally flag, which we put up when in port and which showed everyone that we were part of a fleet. Many of the boats had their own personal boat flag, so I decided to make one. We bought a huge white sheet of material and I drew on the boat name, a rainbow and a dolphin, which I later painted.

It wasn't until it had been up a few days and it had got wet in the rain, that all the colours started to run on it. I guess the paints weren't waterproof after all....oops.

10th June 1999

The rally organisers had organised a dinghy race between the yachts today so we spent the afternoon preparing the dinghy, decorating it with flags and filling it with flower bombs. We all dressed up in black clothes, applied war paint and wore bandanas on our heads. We had a spare emergency dinghy stored below deck, so we decided to get it out as it came with a mast and sail. We weren't allowed to use the sail as that would have been cheating, so instead we used some wind scoops off the boat and decorated the mast with flags. Wind scoops were made from a lightweight tent type material and acted like a wind funnel. They were used on the boat over the forward and stern hatches to help guide the wind down and into the boat. We actually had quite an advantage over the others as we were able to use the wind to speed us up, while the others were just rowing. We nearly came first but unfortunately as we decided to throw flour bombs at the judge (one of the rally organisers) we were disqualified.

14th June 1999

After a couple more nights of beach barbecues with the other yachts, we set sail for Fiji. It was a short three-day sail to the island of Vanua Levu where we moored stern-to outside Savusavu Yacht Club. We were welcomed in by the yacht club who greeted us with a lovely fresh basket of fruit and a yacht club flag. Even the customs guys were a pleasure to have onboard, everyone seemed so friendly. We got chatting to one of the officers about our ever-expanding collection of used phone cards and he later returned with over 500. This doubled what we had already so we were thrilled. He had been collecting for a few years and was really happy to give his collections to some young girls. We were over the moon and the Fijian cards were some of the most beautiful we had seen.

The next day the yacht club put on a local feast for the rally boats and some great traditional Fijian dancing.

Some local Fijian children

Over the next few days we caught up on schoolwork and took advantage of having access to fresh running water, so we gave the boat a good clean.

One night when we were sleeping onboard we were suddenly woken by loud bangs coming from the back of the boat. We were stern-to the dock and as the wind had picked up we had dragged anchor causing us to get pushed into the dock. We quickly tied ourselves onto the neighbouring boat, but on doing so we caused them to drag their anchor. Now they were smashing against the dock too. They needed to reset their anchor so they started pulling it up, but on doing so found that their anchor was somehow wrapped around a mooring buoy. They were unable to free it in the dark and had no choice but to leave it until the morning and re-moor next to us. Adrenalin was pumping through our bodies while we were running about on deck in our pyjamas trying to quickly re-moor the boat in the strong winds while the girls were at the back with fenders fending off the boat. After re-anchoring the anchor was now holding up, so our neighbours tied off on us until the morning.

The plan was to leave the next day but on starting the engine we found out that the alternator had packed up. This was the only method we had to charge the boat batteries instantly. Without it we had no way on charging them so it needed to be sorted before we left. So Dad cracked on with fixing it for the rest of the day.

We then headed to a lovely bay along the coast and decided to go snorkelling. The water was very clear so we were able to see lots of fish. Dad bought a disposable underwater camera but there was so many fish that he used the film up in about five minutes.

24th June 1999

We had a lovely easy night's sail to the next island, Suva, the capital of Fiji. Suva was a surprisingly large city. It was quite busy and the harbour was full of boats. We went straight ashore to take a look around the shops. They seemed to be cheap and we ended up coming back with an electric fan for the saloon, a new video player as the previous one had now packed up and an exercise machine so Dad could start exercising onboard to get fit. As usual we asked around local shops for any used telephone cards and one shop told us about a local Chinese man who had a collection of over 100,000 cards. We got in touch with him and he invited us into his house to make some trades. He was trying to give us some quite rare phone cards and wanted at least 10 cards for one of his. We did quite a bit of trading and at the end of the day managed to get most of the Fijian cards ever printed, however we felt a little ripped off as he was a professional and took most of our good swops leaving us with a collection that was quite small.

The lady whose boat had sunk was still with the rally and had been taking turns living onboard other rally boats. Dad invited her to stay with us for a bit so she took my bottom bunk for a few days. It was fun having a guest onboard as it made a change from just being a family. She also brought some different foods with her and the tastiest muesli cereal which got eaten and finished on the first day as we all had some.

We slowly sailed around the south coast of Fiji, stopping off at Vunaniu Bay before heading to Natadola Harbour. On the way we fished with the rod and reel and managed to catch two lovely three-foot dorados at the same time. Both reels went off at once so we must have gone through a large school of fish. We didn't know which line to deal with first and we didn't want to get them tangled around each other so we brought them in separately.

Natadola was very peaceful and had a stunning white sand beach that seemed to go on for miles. We had heard that the locals did horse rides ashore so Dani and Corrie went for a ride along the long beach there.

After Natadola we sailed 25 miles to the west towards Musket Cove Resort off the 400-acre island of Malolo Lailai. The weather was rough, gusting 30-35 knots, which made it nearly impossible to navigate safely through the hidden reefs. The resort kindly sent a guide boat out to guide us in through the dangerous reef. We moored stern-to the dock with our bow attached to a mooring.

With around 12 km of untouched beaches on Malolo Island, three popular tourist resorts and an airstrip, this little island had quite a few tourists and heaps of young kids. We were able to use the facilities ashore including the trampolines, kids parks, swimming pools and they even had a bit of a dance club at one of the other welcoming resorts which we visited regularly. We made friends pretty quickly with the tourists and other yachtie kids, so every day after school we rushed off the boat to the other resorts and spent the afternoon playing games and having fun with the children and teens there. As the whole island was very safe Mum and Dad allowed us to go out whenever we wanted without accompanying us.

Not far from where the boat was moored there was a small gift shop which sold a selection of sweets and chocolate, so every day we took a trip to buy some soft mints with our pocket money.

So many tourists also meant lots of telephone boxes and lots of used phone cards lying around. Most days we were able to pick up around 50 so our collection was rapidly expanding again and so were our duplicates for trading. We left plastic containers out by a few phones asking people to put their used ones in there and every few hours we went to check on them.

Quite a few of the rally boats were leaving the rally for good in Fiji and going on their own adventure so we hosted a bit of a goodbye party for them. We had got to know some of them quite well so it was rather sad saying goodbye knowing that we would probably never see them again.

Musket Cove had a hi-speed catamaran that regularly made trips to the town of Nadi on the mainland so one day we went for a bit of a ride. Wow, what a difference a faster engine made. What would have taken a good few hours on Rainbow Spirit only seemed to take a few minutes on this high-speed cat. When we arrived there we spotted another rally boat in the marina getting some serious repairs done. We went to say hi and they told us that a few days before they had hit one of the many reefs off Fiji and had nearly sunk. It made us think about how easily you could lose your home just by a minor navigation error.

From here we took a taxi to the second largest town in Fiji, Lautoka, where we spent the day shopping at the market for groceries. We picked up some plastic boxes for our phone cards to store them in as we had been using hand-made cardboard boxes which weren't so strong. Lautoka, also known as Sugar City, was the centre of the sugar industry in Fiji so we saw many large trucks transporting sugar cane through the town centre.

Over the next few days some of the rally boats started leaving the marina. We waved one of our friends off the dock and they started to make their way out when all of a sudden they came to a standstill. They seemed to have lost all power in the engine. They quickly fended themselves off the other boats that the wind was blowing them onto and came back in to the dock. They couldn't figure out what had happened.

But on closer inspection they had found that their propeller had come off. They had previously had it cleaned or serviced in another port and the person who put it back on hadn't tightened the nut that was holding it on enough. The nut had come off completely and as soon as the boat was put into gear, the propeller then flew off, leaving the boat with no prop. Luckily it happened when they were leaving the marina and not while they were navigating through some dangerous reef. They got a diver down to find the propeller parts, had it fixed and were soon on their way again.

14th July 1999

We had been in Fiji for over 10 weeks, slowly cruising around the coastline on Viti Levu and neighbouring islands and it was time to head off on our next leg of the trip, towards Vanuatu, a four-day sail away.

On the second day we got stuck in a mini weather system which gave us wet weather and wind for the whole day. The Bimini wasn't as waterproof as it used to be so whoever was in the cockpit got a little wet. It was cold and miserable being on watch. Luckily after a day the trough passed and we were back to sunny weather again. The wind completely died on us then so the remaining two days we spent motoring.

We had a little visitor en route to Vanuatu. A huge moth flew down into the boat to take a rest. It was rather big and was a beautiful brown and orange colour. It reminded us of the colours of autumn so we decided to name it Season. We weren't too sure what to feed it so we mixed a bit of water with some sugar, which it seemed to love.

Me and Dani shared two-hour watches to keep each other company but as we were motoring most of the way there wasn't too much to do on watch so we decided to take it in turns to sleep for 20 minutes while the other one looked out. This actually made the watch pass so much quicker.

My Round the World Journal

18th July 1999

We motored into Port Villa, the largest city and capital of Vanuatu on the island of Efate. We were told to moor straight on the quarantine buoy while we checked in at customs. As Malaria was quite bad on the island and we weren't taking any malaria tablets, we took extra care to not get bitten. We gave the boat a good spray, put mozzie nets on all the hatches and windows, dressed in long sleeved tops and trousers and sprayed any remaining skin with repellent.

As soon as customs and immigration inspected the boat, we went ashore to explore the many shops. The town spread up the steep hillsides of the harbour which overlooked the beautiful lagoon we were anchored in. The people were very friendly and happy and made us feel very welcome in their country. We visited duty-free shops; fresh fruit markets and a local market where the local women were sewing colourful clothes and materials on hand operated sewing machines.

We found a card trader in one of the shops who traded some cards with us and we were chuffed to have some Vanuatu cards in our collection.

20th July 1999

After only two days in Vanuatu, we fuelled up and left for Australia. Dad allowed me to drive the boat off the fuel dock for the first time, so that was rather exciting.

There was still very little wind out at sea, not enough wind to fill the headsail, so instead we put up our spare yankee sail on the inside forestay. This sail was a lot smaller so we were hoping that it would at least catch some wind but it was a waste of time so we took it back down.

Dani had managed to complete her term's schoolwork so it was only me and Corrie doing schoolwork now, which we were slightly envious about. It gave us the extra push to crack on with it and get it done so that we could look forward to some time off in Australia.

Dani kept herself busy and offered to sort out my stamp collection which had become a bit of a mess over the past year collecting new stamps in each port.

On the second day the wind started to pick up so we were able to sail properly again and switch off our motor. We were managing to make very good speed, averaging 8-9 knots, as we were on our fastest point of sail with the headsail poled out and the wind slightly behind us. We had a few birds land on the boat for the night to take a bit of a rest and as soon as dawn broke they flew off.

As the days went on the wind picked up and so did the seas. We got a gale warning through our seasat news instrument which Dad brought up on the computer. We spoke to the yachts that were a day or so ahead of us and they were getting 35-50 knots of wind. We were in for a bit of a storm ahead so we decided to put the storm jib up before it got too rough to go on deck. We decided to change course to help avoid it so ended up missing the worst part but we still got 35-knot winds and rough seas.

Me, putting up the storm jib

Visibility was unbelievably bad due to the rain and it became dangerous not being able to see about 50 metres ahead. Dad wanted us to take extra care looking out for ships on watch so he promised us USD$10 for every ship we spotted. We prepared a flare in the cockpit just in case we spotted one on collision course for us. These ships are often so big that they don't see small yachts at all. In the past, container ships have pulled into port to find parts of yachts and masts stuck on the front of their ship. These large ships also came up on you very fast. They travel at least three times faster than us and if we spotted one in this poor visibility heading towards us then it probably would have been too late to do anything. Luckily we didn't spot any.

After a few days the clouds cleared up and the sun finally came out. We still had quite high winds and the seas were a little choppy but we were just glad it wasn't raining anymore. Dad went to turn on the inverter box which fed the plugs on the boat with electric, but it wouldn't work, so we were unable to boot the computer to check the forecast. Luckily we were only one day off landfall.

Samantha Saunders

Chapter 12
The Land of Oz

Australian customs were very strict about what we brought into the country and were known to do thorough checks onboard. We had to get rid of certain cans of meat and foods before entering Australia so we had every cupboard open, seat and floorboard up checking every can and package. We tossed the contents of them overboard, of course throwing the empty cans in the bin.

We even locked up our alcohol as you weren't allowed to consume brought in drinks while travelling in Australia.

While we had our head under the floorboards we kept hearing this strange clicking noise and couldn't figure out what it was. Dad thought maybe something had got caught under the boat and was now lightly banging on the hull. It was a little bit freaky as we had no clue what it could be. It wasn't until we went on deck that we found ourselves surrounded by a beautiful school of dolphins. We had never heard them like that before but I guess the noise travelled through the water and into the hull.

29th July 1999

After nine days at sea we reached landfall. I don't know what it was about Australia but we girls were definitely excited. I'm not sure whether we were looking forward to the huge shopping malls or the fresh milk more.

After checking in on the customs dock at Yorkeys Knob Marina in Cairns and customs doing their very thorough check of the boat (they even had a look in the toilet and under the boat's headboards) we made our way into the marina. It was really windy and we had difficulty getting into the tight berth as the wind kept taking the stern in a direction of its own. Luckily we were there ready with fenders so not too much damage was done.

The yacht club was ultra-modern so we went straight ashore and Dad treated us all to a nice lunch. It kind of felt like we were back in Europe or the UK again, but on a very hot summer's day. After lunch I took a ride into town with Jen who wanted to check her emails at an Internet café. I had heard of the Internet but had never been on it before so when I sat down at the computer there, I was a bit puzzled on what to do. Everyone around me seemed to be experts with this new technology, typing away and clicking on things. Jen suggested searching for something interesting such as phone card collections and print a couple of pages out, so I started to use Google for the first time and explore websites. What I didn't realise was that some of these web pages when printed consisted of more than five pages, and for the next hour I was happy printing every page I came across. It wasn't until I left the café that I was handed an expensive bill of around USD$20 for the printing. That was nearly two months of pocket money so I wasn't too impressed.

As Cairns was one of the stop off points on the Rally, the organisers were there to welcome each boat in and host some parties and events for us all. It was nice being able to catch up with everyone again and also to see the other kids from the rally.

Dad hired a car straight away so we could take a trip into town every day. The shops were great and there were many chandleries for Dad to get boats parts from. Corrie and I had now finished our term's work so we were on holiday until September when the new year started. We got stuck into cleaning the boat thoroughly, the usual polishing of the decks, hull and stainless which were now showing signs of rust again after having saltwater on it for so long. In the afternoons we took trips to the shops and did some sightseeing. We ended up coming back with a brand new bread maker one day. We had started to get a bit tired of making our own bread at sea, especially when it was rough and had heard from the other boats how amazing the bread tasted from the bread makers. And oh my gosh they were right, it had to be the best tasting bread we had ever had. So fresh and warm when cooked that the butter instantly melted on it, not to mention the wonderful smell it gave off while baking. The only problem was that it tasted a little too good. We could easily get through a whole loaf just for a snack.

We found an electrician to fit a new inverter but after three hours it packed up again, along with the TV this time. There must have been something seriously wrong with the electrics somewhere. Maybe saltwater had leaked into the boat somehow corroding the cables.

Me with a kangaroo

Not too far away from the marina was Tjapukai Aboriginal Park which was a tourist attraction that allowed people to experience and learn about the aboriginal culture. It included performances and dances, traditional food, clothing, shops, art and tools. We learned how to throw boomerangs and how to play a didgeridoo, although it was a practiced skill so none of us could get the hang of it. From there we headed by car to a nearby crocodile farm where we got to meet some of the local animals and stroke and feed some tame kangaroos. This was the first time any of us had ever seen a kangaroo so it was quite magical. We were even more excited when we saw a mother kangaroo with a young joey in her pouch.

8th August 1999

We travelled a little further in the car today to the Atherton Tablelands and ended up on a muddy very bendy lane through forests which we travelled on for miles. We came across our first giant termite hill along with termites at the side of the road. How such little critters could build such a strong and large structure was fascinating. We visited the famous Kauri twins that were very large trees in the Hardy Forest accessed by boardwalks. We saw the cathedral fig tree that was more than 500 years old and we came across the Tinaroo Dam which was a hydro power station that created electricity. It was so interesting that we ended up spending a few hours exploring it.

One of the many termite hills

12th August 1999

The boat hadn't been out of the water for more than a year by now and the antifouling on the bottom needed a serious re-paint. It had chipped and rubbed off in places and weed had started to stick to these bare spots. So out of the water Rainbow Spirit came. The crane was a lot larger than the one we had used previously in Trinidad, but then again this boat yard had much larger boats. The yard was so busy that there was actually no space for us to fit in line with the other yachts on the hard, so they plonked us down in the middle of the yard's road.

We spent the next few days cleaning the boat thoroughly. Dani and I had already cleaned the hull a few days before, but doing it in the choppy water of the Marina had made it difficult. It was quite a pain tightly hanging on to the side of the boat in the dinghy while the other person cleaned. You only needed to get one spot of water on the hull while you were polishing for it to get messed up. The hull had to be stone dry to do a proper job and not to leave streaks and smudge marks.

With the boat being out of the water you could now see all the marks we had missed. We persuaded Dad that it would be a great idea to get it professionally cleaned by people who had all the tools and equipment instead. He agreed and they did the best job ever. The hull looked like it had come out of a show room. The guy who did it tried to persuade Dad to get the name of the boat painted onto the bow, but when the quote came back at more than £1000 we decided to leave it.

We had all of the old antifouling scraped off and some fresh coats applied. We decided to again move the water line of the antifouling up so that it now covered more of the hull. This was because most of the time we were heavily stocked up on fuel, water and food so the boat was sitting a bit lower underneath the water than usual.

We had taken up the hobby of rollerblading and as the yard had so much concrete around, it was great to practise on. Dad had bought Dani a pair of new blades for her upcoming birthday and another woman on the rally had a spare pair so we took to rollerblading in the evenings. At first it was impossible to do, but after a week or so we got much better. Dani even started doing jumps being the dare devil she was.

We visited the Kuranda Scenic Railway and Skyrail on one weekend. This was one of the most unique railways in Australia consisting of traditional tin carriages which meandered through lush green rainforest, rugged mountains, waterfalls and the pretty colourful village of Kuranda. Dad also booked us on a four-wheel drive adventure with a local tour guide called Berny which was thrilling and exciting.

On the Kuranda Scenic Railway

20th August 1999

It was Dani's 13th birthday today so Dad took us into town to walk around the malls there and have a go at ice-skating. It was the first time any of us had been and was quite a bit different than the rollerblades we were used it.

The next day we headed north to Port Douglas, another marina along the coast that was surrounded by forest and coral reefs. It was the only place on earth where two world heritage listed jewels existed - the Great Barrier Reef and the Daintree Rainforest. Port Douglas was also known for its four mile golden sand beach.

We had heard that there was a good doctor in Port Douglas and as Dani and I had started to get terrible teenage skin, we thought maybe the local doctor could recommend something. Unfortunately she wasn't very sympathetic and told us to go on the pill to help our skin which Dad found very funny and said no way was that happening.

It had been a while since our rigging had been checked so Dad organised some riggers to come onboard to inspect it. They also added some foldaway steps on each side of the mast leading up to the first set of spreaders. We thought that this would come in handy if we ever needed to quickly climb up to free something but didn't want the hassle of setting up the bosun's chair and hoist. It would also come in handy while navigating through dangerous reefs because the higher you were, the better view you had of the rocks below the water line.

We prepared the boat to leave in the marina for a couple weeks as we were going on a family adventure. As we packed up our suitcases and bikes in the back of the four-wheel drive, we were excited to be doing something different. We went straight to the Daintree National Park where we were shown around by a great tour guide. Then it was on to the famous Mossman Gorge where the Mossman River passed over huge granite boulders which lined the river creating swimming holes. We took the Daintree ferry across the Daintree River before arriving at our guesthouse for the night. The owners had put on an evening meal for us and told us about a nearby waterfall which we went to check out the next day. They lived on a bit of a farm because they had animals roaming around, lots of chickens and ducks which made us a little home sick for the farm back home in Wales.

We then set off on a drive to Cooktown named after the famous James Cook (Captain Cook). On the way we spotted wild kangaroos and dingos. It was amazing to see these in the wild. It may have been normal to the locals but they fascinated us.

We came across some black rocky hills composed of granite which were named the Black Mountains. We found this amusing as we were from the Black Mountains in Wales in the UK and we had now come across some more black mountains on the other side of the world. Of course we had to take lots of family shots by them to send to family and friends back home.

At the Black Mountain National Park

In Cooktown there was an old museum which was having a closing down sale at the time. We ended up buying souvenirs, sharks jaws, collections of butterflies, a lovely painted didgeridoo. We told them we would pick it all up in the boat when we sailed past in a few weeks.

From Cooktown we took a 300 km drive through bush, deserts and rivers and came across termite hills even bigger than before. There were snakes and wallabies everywhere, including many dead ones which had been run over which was sad to see. We stayed in beautiful bird lodges and other sites near to crocodiles.

The terrain kept changing, one day we were driving through lush green forests, the next we were in dry and barren deserts. The desert roads were made from sand tracks and with the wind and the large road trains constantly going over them, some of the roads formed ridges in them for miles and miles. This made the whole ride very bumpy indeed, so bumpy that it started to gives us a headache. What a relief it was when the road flattened out.

One of the many road trains, some even had four trailers

As we had our bikes with us we took it in turns in the mornings to set off a bit earlier than the car and start cycling. Then an hour or so later Mum would come past in the car and scoop us up. Dad and I were cycling one day when little whirlwinds started blowing around us, picking up the leaves in their path. We cycled on and they disappeared.

3rd September 1999

Our short adventure was soon over and it was time to head back to the boat, but what an awesome adventure it had been.

We set off with Rainbow Spirit towards Cooktown, which was a couple of hours sail north. Dani jumped ship for the day and joined a friend's boat, which she enjoyed. When we arrived we went straight onshore to pick up our pieces we had bought a few days earlier from the museum. We got chatting to the lovely lady there and ended up inviting her and her nine-year old son back to the boat for the evening.

While we were in Cooktown we were told a story of a woman called Mary Watson who lived on nearby Lizard Island in the 1880s with her husband, baby and two Chinese workmen. One day while her husband was away at sea on his fishing boat some mainland aborigines attacked Lizard Island. One workman was killed with spears and the other one was injured. Mary fired a gun which scared them off. She then gathered up a small supply of water and food and fled the island with her baby and injured workman in an iron tank in hope she would get picked up by a passing vessel. She kept a diary during the passage and a few months later both bodies were found in the iron tank washed up in the mangroves. The last entry to her diary ended with "No water. Near dead with thirst". So she must have died of thirst, which was rather sad to hear. Cooktown still had the iron tank which we went to check out after we had heard the story.

Overlooking the anchorage were two lovely viewpoints and a lighthouse which we took a hike up to. We took some distant photos of Rainbow Spirit in the anchorage down below.

It was very windy in the small anchorage. There were shallows all around us and we couldn't risk the boat swinging around on the anchor in the night and ending up on one of the many banks, so we decided to put a stern anchor out to keep us in position.

Next stop was Lizard Island, a national park on the Great Barrier Reef and named by Captain Cook in 1770 after him finding lots of lizards there. En route we caught the largest barracuda yet but unfortunately due to the reef poisoning it would have been dangerous to eat so we had to throw it back. We hated wasting it especially after we had killed the poor thing.

Quite a few of the rally boats were anchored off Lizard Island so we organised a hike to a nearby mountain top called Cook's Lookout. This was a good 3-4 hour hike to the top and back over uneven and loose rocks. We spotted two very huge lizards on the way up.

Another day was spent on the beach having a mini sports day with fun activities and games. We had to keep an eye out for salt water crocodiles in the area so we didn't swim too far out to sea.

We were bored one day and the crew on one of the other boats who were keen racers decided to hop onboard for the day and help set up our spinnaker. Our spinnaker had never been used and it was a little too big for us to manage as a family. It also needed very light winds to fly and on this day the weather was just perfect, so we up-anchored and sailed out to sea. We got it out and took some photos from the dinghy. Dad had originally designed the colours on it and had tried to make it as colourful as possible after the boat name Rainbow Spirit.

14th September 1999

We spent a week or so hopping up the anchorages on the coastline while travelling up north.

Today we went through the famous Albany Passage, which was at the very top of Australia and was known for its rip tides, currents and tricky navigation. We had to time it exactly right so that the tide would be travelling with us and we passed through with 2.5 knots of current pushing us from behind. We spotted lots of very large turtles mating on the way so we guessed it must have been mating season.

With our spinnaker up

That evening we pulled into Red Island which had a small shop so we took advantage of stocking up on some fresh milk. We were getting low on water on the boat and a campsite there kindly allowed us to fill up with water from one of their hosepipes. There was no dock so we made several trips back and forth in the dinghy with jerry cans.

16th September 1999

We were on our way to Darwin, a five-day sail west around the north coast of Australia. The first few days were calm so we ended up motoring quite a bit. It was very calm below deck so we cracked on with schoolwork as we were now into a new school year and term. I had been trying to get through my French course book but was struggling with it a bit. I found it hard not being able to practise it out loud and it was impossible to get the pronunciation right. One of the other boats had a lovely man onboard who was fluent in several languages, so in the evenings he began to give me some French lessons over the radio and corrected me on my pronunciation.

We nearly had a little visitor en route to Darwin. We spotted a large snake off the stern of the boat that started swimming towards us. It was very fast indeed. But when we all started making a commotion on deck shouting out for mum to come up to look, it dived down and disappeared.

21st September 1999

We arrived into Cullen Bay Marina in Darwin late afternoon after spending the morning navigating through passages and reefs. We were buzzed again by a plane, but this time we remembered to put our VHF radio on so were able to hear them calling straight away.

There was so much tide in Darwin that the marina had to be kept inside a gated lock. Each yacht that entered had to go in and out through a lock so a time slot had to be booked up ahead of time. There had also been a bit of a problem with a rampant shell fish/mollusc bug in the area that could take over all the pipes in the boat, so before we went through we had some fisheries staff come onboard to put disinfectant down our seacocks and toilets. Seacocks were taps in the bottom of the hull that allowed water or liquids to pass in and out.

27th September 1999

After a week of jobs onboard and getting ahead with schoolwork Dad decided to take us on another road trip, so we packed our suitcases again, jumped in a hired car and headed out to Kakadu National Park and the Mary River Wetlands.

That evening we checked into our accommodation for the night and were pleasantly surprised that the guest rooms were very large luxury tents with proper beds and everything inside. It almost felt like we were camping, but this was very luxurious camping. It was great being inside the tent and being able to hear the many birds and parrots that surrounded the area.

Our posh tents

We were very close to a crocodile lookout point overlooking a large lake full of crocodiles so we went to check that out and some were unbelievably huge. They sat low below the water with only their eyes popping out so you had to look very closely to spot them.

Just down the road was a billabong full of local bird life and wildflowers along with Ubirr Rock, another World Heritage site. This was famous for its rock art and very old aboriginal art paintings on the rocks and walls. The views from the tops were impressive with a good 360 degree view of the surrounding floodplains and cliffs, not to mention a great sunset which we stayed to watch.

Some of the roads between the sights were very long and unmarked and we ended up getting lost on more than one occasion. We ended up passing the same spot twice before realising that we must be going in circles. Many parts of the road were blocked by low lying rivers which you could easily pass over in a four-wheel drive when the river was low.

If it rained then it became dangerous so we were keen to get a move on each time we got lost, just in case it started raining heavily and we got stuck in the middle of nowhere....surrounded by crocs.

Chapter 13
Towed into Bali

3rd October 1999

It was time to move on and so we left Darwin and headed for Bali in Indonesia with most of the other rally boats.

It was only a nine-day sail away but we ended up hitting patches of flat seas and no wind at all, so we had to motor for most of the way. We stayed within sight of one of our friends' boats so we had company en route and chatted to them daily on the radio.

The sea was calm and still so one day we pumped up the dinghy on deck, put it in the water with the outboard on and motored over to our friends' boat for a cup of tea mid ocean. This was a little amusing because we left mum and Corrie in charge onboard board Rainbow Spirit.

A few days later there was still no wind and our friends were now getting very low on fuel. They did not have enough fuel if we continued motoring the rest of the way so for a couple of days we decided to tow them behind so they could reserve some. For some reason even though our boats were similar sizes we had a much larger fuel tank than them so we could hold more and go longer distances.

After talking over our plan on how to tow them we motored alongside their boat so they could pass their line to us, but somehow we hit them on a bad angle. Their boat swung around and our anchor ended up hitting their deck and somehow got caught on their side rail. We were now pushing them head on into their side with our anchor. It all happened rather quickly and after lots of panicking and shouting we quickly released the anchor and we were free. It just goes to show that even in super calm weather things could still go wrong very quickly at sea. Luckily no one was hurt, just their deck was scratched where our anchor had hit it. We had more luck with the second attempt, this time approaching each other at a much slower speed. We towed them for two days so they could now chill out for a bit and get some rest. They only had two crew onboard so they must have been a lot more tired than us.

During the trip we saw water snakes, whales, dolphins, turtles and so many fishing boats. We constantly had to avoid them and their trailing nets which went on for miles. It probably wouldn't have been so bad if we were sailing, because if we did ever go over any of their nets it might have been okay. But as we were running the engine there was a high chance that it could have fouled the prop. There would have been no way to free it as there was no way any of us could have dived down and cut it from the hull and propeller. We kept a very close eye out for nets and boats the whole trip.

One of our rally friends once got caught up in a net when they were sailing the Atlantic. They had no choice but to jump in the water mid ocean and cut it off, it was a nightmare for them.

A mummy and baby dolphin, swimming at the bow

With all the motoring we were doing we found that our engine starting having difficulty and was struggling a little. It didn't seem to be getting enough fuel for some reason and ended up conking out a few times. This was rather scary and we had to get it fixed fast as we were only a few days from Bali. We found out that the fuel filter was so filthy with this thick sludgy gunk that it was becoming clogged and unable to feed a clean supply of fuel fast enough to the engine. We changed the filter but within a few hours of motoring the same thing happened again. It was getting a bit silly having to turn the engine off every few hours and clean the filters out. I think we had picked up a fuel bug which made the fuel turn into a thick sludge and as our fuel tanks were getting lower and lower, the sludge which must have settled at the bottom of the tank was beginning to be used up. As we neared land the problem seemed to get worse and it cut out more often. And if things couldn't get any worse, our furling line which pulled the headsail in and out had also broken so we were without a headsail. This was becoming very stressful and we were nearing land by the hour. We had strong wind, rough seas, reverse currents and rip tides coming into Bali and we had no choice but to get towed by our friends. Thank goodness that they were travelling with us.

After being towed into the marina and tying off to the nearest pontoon we all stopped to take a deep breath. We were relieved that we had made it in safely.

After being in Bali marina for a few hours we noticed how much dirtier the water was than Australia. It may have just been the direction of the currents but the water was brown and the marina had quite a lot of rubbish floating around the boats. We even came across a dead goat in the water which was rather swollen and smelly.

20th October 1999

After thoroughly cleaning the boat's fuel tanks out, replacing the fuel filters, filling them back up with fresh clean fuel and getting the engine up and running again, we decided to take some time off to do some exploring in Bali.

We had been to Bali on holidays before so we knew our way around quite well. We headed for Kuta, the most touristy part, and booked ourselves into our favourite hotel from years before. But when we got there it was surprisingly run down so we immediately checked out and found a newer hotel down the road that happened to have 50 percent off on their room rates. Dad booked a family suite that had an upstairs and downstairs which was great as we girls took the upstairs. We felt like we had our own area to hang out in and we absolutely loved it. It was so much more spacious that the small cabins on the boat, not to mention flushing toilets. What a treat it was not to have to pump water out and in every time you went to the bathroom!

Kuta was a buzzing busy little town. During the day the road sides and side streets were full with local market stalls selling all kinds of things including clothing, bags, ornaments, jewellery and souvenirs. At night it turned into a bit of a party heaven for the tourists when the clubs, bars and restaurants came alive.

Bali was extremely cheap to eat out in so we ate out for lunch and dinner. The prices were cheap enough in the market stalls but we still couldn't help trying to barter them down for an even bigger discount. It just made it more fun and you went away feeling like you had grabbed a bargain. We ended up spending all our pocket money on clothes, bags, jewellery and presents for our friends back home, everything was just so cheap.

Right smack bang in the centre of Kuta was a very large water park called Waterbomb which was full of water slides and activities. The weather was fabulous and the water was so warm it felt like you were getting into a warm bath. We had so much fun on the different slides there we didn't want to leave.

We had previously done some white water rafting in Bali years before but Corrie had always been too young to go so she and mum had always missed out. This time we all went as a family which was lovely. After an exciting hour of travelling down a rocky and boisterous river, avoiding rocks, going down waterfalls and hanging on for dear life, we jumped over the side of the dinghy and floated beside it while the calm current took us downstream.

We ended up having such a good time in Kuta that we extended our stay further and ended up being one of the last yachts to leave Bali…….again.

Samantha Saunders

Chapter 14
Indonesia & Malaysia

5th November 1999

We finally left Bali and headed towards Karimun Jawa Island, a very tiny island in a national marine park just off the north coast of Samarang. We overnighted in a few anchorages on the way as it was too dangerous to navigate through the many unlit fishing boats and lobster pots at night. We couldn't risk hitting or getting caught up in one, so we decided it was best to pull in while it was dark. One of the anchorages was so roly that I don't think any of us slept that night. It was so roly for our friends on a nearby boat that they upped anchor in the night and were gone when we woke the next morning.

There seemed to be quite a lot of small fishing boats in this area, some were very inquisitive and headed towards us to check us out. Luckily we had friends on a nearby boat so we kept an eye out for each other in case the fisherman tried to board us.

When we arrived at Karimun Jawa we were starting to get low on water and fuel so we filled up from a small local boat there that brought it from the shore. It was a very slow process as it had to be pumped out by hand.

When we were nicely full we headed onshore to check out the local town there. We took a ride on a bike cart and then went swimming off the local beach. The swim didn't last long though as we found that the water was full of jellyfish.

Filling up with fuel and water

12th *November 1999*

Next port of call was Serutu Island off Karimata, an island around 500 miles further northwest so around three days away. En route we saw a waterspout coming up from the ocean. We were keen to take a closer look so changed course and headed straight for it. By the time we got near to it though, it had disappeared.

The wind was a little all over the place, first on the bow then none at all, so we had the engine on constantly. We decided to do a little tacking so we could try and sail for a bit and rest the engine. We adjusted our course to suit the wind angle more. This lasted a while but eventually it died down so the engine went back on again.

I took advantage of the flat seas and went on the computer to type up my Christmas list, although I think I got a bit distracted because I only ended up doing three hours of schoolwork in the end. I guess it just meant a few hours to catch up on over the weekend.

By the time we got to Serutu the weather had turned and it ended up being too dangerous and rough to enter the anchorage there, so we had to sail straight past and sail into the night with the wind on our nose. We were looking forward to giving the motor some rest and anchoring for the night but we had no choice but to continue on. We kept a very close eye out for unlit lobster pots and fishing nets.

Our friend on a neighbouring boat had run his engine so much that he was starting to boil his batteries. He couldn't find a way to stop the engine from putting power into them through the alternator, so he was starting to panic a bit. Acid had bubbled out of them and they were now drying out quite rapidly. He was worried that he would boil them dry and they may explode or something. There was a horrible acid and burning smell working its way through his boat and he had no battery water left to put in them. Dad tried to help him out over the radio by telling him to cut one of the wires from the alternator that was feeding them with energy. Our friend ummed and ahhed for a bit as he wasn't 100 percent sure which wire to cut. But he had no choice but to just got for it and take a chance. We waited nervously on the other side of the VHF while he cut what he thought was the wire. Luckily he found the right one and it did the job.

17th November 1999

We were rather tired from all the motoring so Dad decided to pull into Lingga Island, where we spent a restful night. It also allowed us to turn the engine off and let it cool down overnight so Dad could do some necessary safety checks on it. All was good and so we then set sail again and headed towards Mesanak.

Today was a bit of a special day as we crossed the equator again. We had just crossed north of it and wouldn't be passing it again for the rest of the trip. We all went down below and watched the GPS position change from South to North. It wasn't very often that Latitude read 00.00.000.

When fishing we usually fished with two lines from the back of the boat, one on a fishing rod on the port side, and the other on a lone reel that was fixed to a post at seating level on the starboard side. Today we fished and as usual the reel line caught a fish, so we decided to take the rod line in first so it didn't tangle. On reeling it in though it suddenly became heavy. We had caught a second fish on this line, so we now had two fish for dinner.

After Mesanak we headed to Nongsa Point Marina on the island of Batam, which was the closest island south of Singapore. It was lovely to be on land again with running water and electricity. The whole island was known for being mosquito free due to it being fumigated on a weekly basis. It was funny because we were all sitting in the cockpit one day moored in the marina wondering where all the smoke was coming from in the bush. We thought the island was on fire until someone told us it was the fumigators.

19th November 1999

There was a lovely swimming pool at the marina so we went to check it out. I ended up leaving my shoes by one of the deck chairs there and as soon as I remembered I went straight back, but they had been taken. That was a bit sad as they were my lovely brown All-star slip on ones which I used nearly every day. My only other sandals were a pair of chunky boys' velcro ones which were not feminine at all.

21st November 1999

We got our dinghy on to the pontoon and gave it a thorough wash out. It was one of those foldaway ones so the plastic floorboards could be folded up and removed. It was filthy under the floorboards after not being cleaned for months. There was an inch of sand and green weed everywhere. We gave it all a really good scrub and then put it back in the water again. The floorboards were quite strong and you could stand on them while on dry land. After we had finished the inside we cleaned the dinghy with some special dinghy and fender cleaner. This got off all the dirt and grime. It looked like new when we had finished.

A couple of the other rally boats had seen what we were doing and offered to pay us if we cleaned theirs, so we did. It was good to get some spending money. Then another boat asked us to clean theirs too, which we were even more pleased about. We cleaned the outside of the dinghy first, then Dani and I both jumped inside the dinghy to scrub the floorboards when all of a sudden we heard a loud crack. The floorboard had split. Oh no we had broken it and now we had to go back to the boat owners and tell them. We felt like crying, we felt so bad but luckily Dad offered to tell them himself. We cleaned the rest of the dinghy for the owner but didn't charge anything as we had broken it. That was the last dinghy we offered to do for anyone.

23rd November 1999

We set off from Nongsa Point towards Sabana Cove, a 5-star marina resort that we were all looking forward to experiencing. On leaving Nongsa Point Marina we were followed out by a few other rally boats. As we were making our way out through the marina entrance we heard one of the boats on the VHF shouting for help. They had somehow gone straight over a submerged fishing net which had fouled their prop and they were now drifting engineless towards the harbour walls. Another boat quickly motored to their rescue only a few metres from the rocks and towed them back in. I'm not sure how we missed the net ourselves. They were following very closely behind and we must have only been metres from it. Or maybe we did go through the net but the rope cutter installed on our prop cut its way through it. We would never know but were just relieved out friends didn't do any damage to their boat. They were saved just in the nick of time.

When we were in the Caribbean we motored straight over a lobster pot with a mooring and it fouled our prop for a few seconds and then the rope cutter did its job and cut through it, leaving a trail of cut up rope in the water behind.

Another time we had just anchored in a large bay in Grenada in the dark and as usual put our engine in reverse to dig the anchor in. We had not spotted one of our lines at the back of the boat which was trailing over the side. All of a sudden the prop fouled itself and we stopped dead in the water. We were in a bit of a panic because it meant that someone would now have to dive underneath the boat and cut it off. I came up with the idea that because it had got tangled round the prop while it was in reverse, maybe if we put it in forward gear that it would slowly unravel itself. Dad gave it a try and put it in forward while I took up the slack of the rope with my hands. Slowly it unravelled itself and a few seconds later the other end of the line was back in my hands. We had freed it…yay. Anyway that time the prop cutter didn't work, I guess it didn't work so well in reverse.

Sabana Cove was up a narrow river which was unusual but meant it was very well protected. My gosh, it had to be one of the nicest marinas you have ever seen. It was 5-star, everything was new and high spec, there were even golf buggies on the pontoons to pick you up and take you to the marina office or restaurant. It had lovely facilities such as a games room, gym, restaurants, jacuzzis, saunas, tennis courts and a very large luxurious swimming pool with water slides. And when things couldn't get any better, Dad found out it was only about USD$10 per night to stay there. We couldn't believe it.

One of the rally organisers was there to take our lines and give us the guided tour of the marina and facilities. It felt like we were on holiday in a luxury resort. Nothing quite like the other marinas we were used to.

We girls got up early so we could get the jobs finished for the day so we could spend the rest of the afternoon in the pool there. We had so much fun on the water slides and playing on the small man-made island in the middle of the large swimming pool accessed by footbridges from the pool's sides.

One evening we took a boat ride down the river to see the fireflies. We turned off our torches so it was pitch black. We started to spot them and the more we looked the more we could see. They were everywhere, in the sky, in the bushes, over the water's edge and flying around us in the boat. We had never seen fireflies before and were amazed by their glow. It was fascinating that a little bug could produce this amount of light. We tried to catch some without any luck.

One morning Mum popped to the marina office ashore. We were bow-to the dock, so to climb ashore we had to climb over the bow rails, step onto the anchor, then onto the dock which was sometimes up to a metre below. On this particular morning the rest of us were sitting down below in the saloon when we heard a faint screaming from outside. "Help!" "Help!" we heard and quickly clambered up on deck to see what was going on. We couldn't see anyone. All of a sudden we heard it again. Poor Mum had slipped off the bow, fallen into the water and was clinging by her fingers to the electric line connecting power to the boat. As she couldn't swim this was a terrifying experience for her. The bow was several metres from the water so it would have been impossible to lift her out that way. The dock wasn't that much closer. I quickly jumped into the dinghy and rowed towards her. She clambered on in and was in a bit of shock. Thankfully someone was around to help her. It was the first man overboard we had on Rainbow Spirit, and we were glad that it happened in a marina.

2nd December 1999

Sabana Cove was a short ferry ride from Singapore, so today we went to check it out for a few days and do some shopping there. That night we checked ourselves into a hotel called the Strand, it was run down and very old. Dad actually felt it might be a little unsafe with such old electrics and could be a fire risk, so the next day we checked into the City Bayview hotel opposite, which was much better.

Singapore was really cheap for electronics so Dad bought quite a few things. Many of the malls were several stories high full of TVs, computers, cameras, printers, and any electronic device you could imagine. They had all the very latest models and at much cheaper prices that the UK. A lot of the stores sold the same thing so we took time to get the best deals possible and barter them down. Dad bought himself a new digital camera which I was chuffed about as it meant I got his old one for my upcoming birthday and Christmas present. I had never had my own camera before, and as digital ones had only just come out, I was looking forward to taking my own photos.

My nan (the one who drank that very special drink of Dani's in the Caribbean) and my best friend from England were coming out so we picked them up from the airport and then did a little more shopping at some of the local markets. In the evening we all caught a ride around the centre on one of the local bike carts to see the bright Christmas lights and scenery. We ended up being taken past Raffles Hotel and secretly wished we were staying there instead.

After a couple of nights in Singapore, we headed back on the ferry to Sabana Cove where we spent a few days chilling out and relaxing by the pool. I now had a digital camera to test out so I spent most of my time taking photos of the girls and my friend by the pool. Digital cameras were a fairly new thing in those days and I just loved how I could take an endless supply of photos then delete the ones which weren't so good.

The fancy 5-star Marina at Sabana Cove

6th December 1999

We sadly waved goodbye to Sabana Cove Marina. It had to be one of the nicest marinas we had been in so far so we were sad to be leaving. We set off in the early morning up the river and into the Strait of Malacca, one of the busiest shipping channels in the world. It was pretty busy but at the same time fascinating to see all the huge tankers and ships. We didn't make it to our destination in time and as the sun was setting we quickly pulled into a small island off Singapore.

As we were about to anchor we saw the police coastguard boat rush over to check us out. We put our smiley faces on and asked if we could stay the night there. They were all very lovely and said we could as long as we took a mooring instead of anchoring so we obliged. It wasn't a small plastic mooring but a huge metal and barnacle infested one and as there was no wind and the tides and currents were coming from all directions, we ended up constantly banging into it with the boat. We didn't want our hull to get all scratched up so we set it free and anchored instead hoping the police coastguard didn't notice.

7*th* December 1999

We set off early the next day before the coastguard spotted us at anchor and we sailed all day and night to Admiral Marina in Port Dickson where we spent one night. During the day my friend joined me on deck for some watches. She thought it was rather exciting sailing along looking out for ships. There were so many ships that night though that Mum and Dad took over all the watches. They had a couple of very close calls with a few of them when they became sandwiched between two huge tankers. One of the tankers even shone a spotlight down on us as we were passing it in the shipping channel. They were so large and powerful that it was actually quite terrifying having them so close to us. You could see the ships so clearly as they had floodlights all over their decks and cargo but we were such a small tiny poorly lit boat that it would have been quite easy for them to miss us. We heard Dad swearing a few times from the cockpit so he must have been very stressed out. The next morning he told us that it really did frighten him and at one point he was scared for his life.

It was nice to arrive in Admiral Marina and chill out for a few hours. Mum and Dad needed some time to wind down and catch up on sleep. Luckily the marina had a lovely swimming pool and restaurant which kept us girls amused.

10*th* December 1999

We set off early again for a two-night sail. We ended up motoring every bit of the way as there was no wind at all and the seas were flat. There weren't as many ships to avoid on this passage so I took some night watches with my friend who was now getting the hang of what the boat lights meant and who had right of way. I was always quite sleepy on night watches but she was wide awake with excitement. There were so many shooting stars and the seas were calm and flat. She hadn't seen a shooting star before so it was quite magical for her.

Two days later we arrived into Pulau Dayang Bunting in Langkawi. The Langkawi island chain consisted of 104 tropical islands which still remained very unspoiled and untouched by tourism. Pulau Dayang Buntung translated into Isle of the Pregnant Maiden. The anchorage there was huge and the scenery was stunning. Lush rainforest and local flora and fauna surrounded the bay. The water was so clear that we jumped overboard to go swimming around the boat. We had heard that there was access to a famous inland lake somewhere nearby so we went to check it out in the dinghy. We could see a dock in the distance so we headed over to it but when we got closer we found that it had been damaged in a storm. There was not much of a dock left so it was totally inaccessible. We were still keen to check out the lake so we ventured around the coastline into the next bay and found another access point. This one took us past a lovely little shop full of trinkets and clothes. It was really cheap. We walked through some woodland full of friendly wild monkeys which we fed with some snacks we had before eventually finding the lake.

Pulau Dayang Buntung Lake

The lake was known to have magical properties for infertile women so lots of locals and tourists came to swim there. They had pedal boats available to hire so we took a few out to have a play.

14th December 1999

This morning we sailed to the main Langkawi Island and dropped anchor off Kuah, Langkawi's largest town and capital. We stopped off for lunch and a swim on the way at another one of Langkawi's many stunning beaches.

The town of Kuah had a huge iconic eagle at its entrance and was full of lots of eating places and shops. For this type of region it seemed to be quite modern so I could understand why flocks of tourists came here every year.

That evening we all went out to eat at the local yacht club ashore as it was my nan and friend's last night. The next morning we waved them off at the airport as they headed towards Singapore on the way back to the UK.

The iconic eagle at Kuah

Chapter 15
Thailand

18th December 1999

After taking a few more days to explore the neighbouring Langkawi islands, we finally set sail for Thailand, which was only a day's sail away. This was the first time we had properly been able to sail since Australia due to the calm wind conditions.

We set off at 6am so managed to arrive into Thailand before nightfall. We anchored off Ko Rok Nok, a tiny uninhabited island in a national park. It had the most beautiful white sand beach and crystal clear blue waters. Dad was trying to get us out exploring, but we girls weren't feeling up to it. I think we had been a little spoiled by all these beaches and all we really wanted was to get to another busy port that had some civilisation, shops and other children to play with. We really didn't want to see yet another abandoned beach. Dad was excited though, he kept telling us to come up on deck and look at the stunning scenery. He eventually managed to persuade us to go ashore and some friends from another rally boat joined us with their windsurfer. We spent a few hours trying to learn to sail it but it was a little too big for us and quite a bit trickier than it looked. You only needed a slight wind and it suddenly took off so it was quite hard to control and a little scary thinking the wind could possibly take you out to sea. That evening we invited the neighbouring boats around to our boat for drinks, but when we heard that there was storm on its way they decided it was best to stay at home and look after their own boats.

19th December 1999

We didn't get any strong winds that night and after taking over an hour to free our anchor chain from one of the many coral heads down below, we set sail for some neighbouring islands just south of Phuket, called Ko Racha Yai. We didn't want to get the chain stuck again so we decided to take a mooring buoy instead, but as there was no wind all the boats on moorings were swinging around hitting each other so we tried to anchor instead. We just couldn't seem to get a hold of anything and kept dragging so in the end we gave up and settled on another mooring further away from the other boats.

Wow, this protected little anchorage and beach looked like it was off a postcard. There were a few small hotel villas and restaurants dotted along the shoreline, but we still found ourselves with the beach to ourselves. It was derelict. We were expecting some of the other rally boats to join us later that day for drinks onboard Rainbow Spirit, but they never arrived so we spent the night chilling out on the boat after eating at the hotel restaurant ashore.

21st December 1999

This morning we headed for Aochalong Bay off the island of Phuket. It was a tricky channel to get in as there were lots of underwater shallows and sand banks coming in which we carefully navigated in high winds. It was very hard to see them and so easy to get stuck but luckily this time we came into the anchorage safe from harm.

We anchored and straight away we spotted a group of kids playing and jumping off a nearby boat. They had a British flag hanging off the back of their boat, meaning that their boat was registered in the UK and they were most likely from the UK too. They must have been looking out for us too because not long after we anchored, the youngsters swam by to introduce themselves. They were a brother and sister from the UK. The girl was the same age as me and her brother was a few years older. They lived on a large traditional looking boat which their parents had built themselves from concrete, yes concrete. You can only imagine how heavy and slow their boat would have been to sail but at the same time very safe if they ever hit anything at sea. Rainbow Spirit was made from fibreglass so was reasonably light but if we ever hit something such as a submerged container or reef, then it was likely that it would have put a hole in her and we would probably sink.

We spent a couple of days here, checking out the local town and trading phone cards with our new friends who were also keen collectors. It was so windy in the anchorage that it was actually quite difficult to get ashore in the dinghy without getting completely drenched. The wind didn't improve and after a couple of days we were ready to leave.

The next port of call was Phi Phi Don, an island a couple of hours sail away which we could clearly see in the distance before setting off. The weather was very windy so dad was quite hesitant trying to leave the dangerous channel. We decided to take a chance as we got in okay so surly getting out would be fine too. We slowly headed out and Dad decided to take the wheel instead of using the autopilot. All of a sudden the depth sounder read. 0.4, 0.3, 0.2, 0.0. We were on the bottom and were stopped dead in our tracks. We had hit a sand bank and the strong wind was now pushing us further on to it. This was quite serious. How on earth were we going to free ourselves? Dad put the engine on full and tried to steer us off and very slowly the boat started to move away from the danger. It was working and eventually after a minute or so of shouting and panic we were free again. It was a close call and we didn't want to risk getting caught on it again. We were all feeling shaken so we decided it was too dangerous to leave today and we headed back into the bay to re-anchor. We girls were secretly chuffed as it meant we could hang out with our new friends for a bit longer.

24th December 1999

It has been four days since the sand bank incident, and it was still blowing in the bay but we were keen to spend Christmas in Phi Phi Don as it was a meeting point for the rally boats and the organisers would be there again. Many of them were already there having pre-Christmas parties, so we set out in windy conditions again. This time we took it very slowly and managed to miss all the sand banks. What a relief it was to be finally out of danger. We had a very bumpy ride to Ton Sai Bay off Phi Phi. It was blowing nearly 40 knots so was very rough.

The little streets of Phi Phi

That evening we went ashore to join in with the fun, on this great little island full of shops, bars, a few dance clubs and loads of restaurants. The buildings were very close together and were separated by narrow sandy paths. We came across local hens and their cute little fluffy chicks. We all stayed out until the early hours of the morning before making our way back to the boat. Dad had one too many drinks, and as he was climbing off the dinghy onto the ladder at the back, he missed the handrail and ended up in the water, which we thought was hilarious. We were glad that it was him who had fallen in and not Mum.

25*th* December 1999

It was Christmas Day so we got up early to open our presents and chilled out on the boat watching movies. Mum cooked a lovely Christmas dinner onboard and then in the evening we met up with the rest of the rally boats and went out for a meal in one of the many restaurants onshore.

For the next couple of days we chilled and relaxed. We left Dad onboard alone for a few hours one day while we went to do some birthday shopping for him.

If you had ever seen the movie 'The Beach" with Leonardo Di Caprio you would remember how beautiful the beach was in it and that beach was literally on the next island of Phi Phi Li, a short taxi boat ride away. I wasn't having such as good day when Dad, Mum, Corrie and Dani went to check it out, so I stayed onboard instead and caught up with my diary. They came back saying how lovely the beach was but how different it looked from the movie. I think they had imported palm trees and vegetation for the movie to make it look quite different.

29*th* December 1999

After five nights in Phi Phi Don, we set sail for Chicken Island off Krabi. Or should I say motored, as there was no wind at all to sail. This was a lovely little place with a white sandspit joining two small islands allowing you to explore both islands. We did a bit of exploring in the kayak and came across a tiny local bar where we stopped to have a drink. Apart from us and a couple of locals, we had the whole beach to ourselves.

Chicken Island, Krabi

30*th* December 1999

The scenery and rock faced cliffs around the area were quite impressive. One had this huge head-like rock protruding out from it. Dad thought it would make a great shot with Rainbow Spirit sailing past, so on our way to the next port, Ao Nang Bay in Krabi about four miles away, we stopped to take photos of Rainbow Spirit sailing.

We spent an hour or so taking photos. Corrie and I went out in the dinghy to take the shots. I was behind the camera and Corrie was steering while Dad motored up and down the mountainous shore line. I bet other yachts and boats in the area wondered what on earth we were doing. It was quite choppy in the dinghy so was quite hard to steady the camera to get a good shot. Unfortunately when we got back to the boat many of the shots were blurry which was disappointing.

As soon as we arrived in Krabi we went ashore to get Dad's hair cut as it was beginning to look a bit out of control….again. We also booked up our tables for the rally's New Year's Eve party which was being hosted at one of the resorts there. It was a buffet with entertainment.

31st December 1999

As Dad was pretty impressed with his new haircut and thought they had done a good job, Mum took us ashore to get the rest of us haircuts. This was a nice little treat and smartened us all up for the New Year's Eve party. In the evening we headed to the resort all smartly dressed up in our best clothes. We had a lovely buffet dinner with live music, classical Thai dancing and fireworks. Dad had managed to get a hold of some Chinese crackers and set some off under the tables of our friends a few times, making everyone scream and jump. Most of the people found it amusing but others not so amusing as it had slightly burnt their feet.

Afterwards we headed to the beach to watch everyone set off Chinese lanterns in the sky. There must have been thousands and thousands of them all along the coastline. The sky looked stunning and as there was no wind they just gently drifted on up into the atmosphere.

We headed home at 1am but some of the youngsters invited me back out with them. They were all a little older and were drinking but as I was only 15 I was a little too young to get involved so one of them brought me home around 3am while the others partied on.

1st January 2000

The adults were rather hung-over and we girls were rather tired from not having much sleep so we got up quite late. One of the youngsters came over with his favourite hangover cure, a Bloody Mary. So he and Dad had a drink or two. It was Dad's birthday so after opening his presents at around 5pm he invited all the other rally boats over. There had never been so many people onboard Rainbow Spirit. I think we counted around 43 people in the end.

2nd December 2000

Phi Phi Don had left quite an impression on us all. It was a very unique and special place unlike the other islands we had visited. The scenery in the large anchorage was stunning so we headed back there for a few more nights. Corrie jumped ship for the day and sailed alongside us on our friend's boat. She found this quite exciting and enjoyed herself.

We spent a couple of more nights here and were so impressed with the scenery that Dad sent me and Corrie out in the dinghy to take some more shots of Rainbow Spirit sailing past. Unfortunately they didn't come out as well as I had hoped so we were unable to use any.

We then went onto Ao Chalong Bay again (the bay where we hit the sand bank). We needed to fill up with fuel and stock up on food from the local supermarket. It was still really windy in the anchorage and as there was no fuel dock to moor next to and fill up, it meant that we had to jerry can the fuel back to the boat. Dad and I clambered in the dinghy with eight empty jerry cans and motored ashore. It was very choppy and the waves were surprisingly large so we took our time. We filled up the containers from a local fuel pump and then made our way back towards the boat in the dinghy. The waves were so choppy and the extra weight of the fuel was dragging the dinghy down in the water. Water started coming over the back of the dinghy and we were starting to sink. More waves came over the sides and we were getting completely soaked from head to toe. There was now a foot of water in the dinghy. I quickly bailed the water out as fast as I could and we arrived back at Rainbow Spirit just in time. We were completely soaked with salt water so had to take showers and put on clean clothes.

We all then headed ashore to the local Tesco supermarket to stock up on food. Yes that's right Tesco, a well-known British chain supermarket that we were very familiar with from back home. It was a fairly large shop so we were able to stock up on quite a bit of food. We had so much that we really didn't want to risk sinking the dinghy again or wetting any food so we jumped in a local water taxi which got us all to the boat in one dry trip.

5th *January 2000*

Today was my 15th birthday and after opening my pressies and cards we headed further along the coast to Patong Beach. Patong was notorious for its nightlife and lady boys and the centre of all action in Phuket. Mum and Dad had bought a birthday cake for later on in the day but we ended up eating it for breakfast instead, oops.

Patong town was dotted with shops, restaurants, clubs, bars and side stalls. We bought heaps of things including clothing, jewellery and movies. We came across a well-equipped dive shop that had a nice collection of snorkelling gear in all different colours so we all upgraded ours. I carefully chose flippers, snorkel and goggles in matching fluorescent yellow. We ended up buying so much that the store threw in some netted snorkel bags for free. These would keep everything organised and together on the boat. That evening we walked around the town checking out the party scene and drunken tourists. We came across a beautiful man with breast implants out on show. Tourists were getting photos with him for a small fee. It was quite an eye opener to say the least. It was hard to tell that he was actually a man as he was so feminine looking.

9th January 2000

We spent a couple of more days in Patong before setting sail for Sri Lanka, a large island south of India and about a week's sail away.

The wind this time was directly behind us so we goose-winged for most of the day. This was a fairly gentle position but it meant that the boat rocked and rolled about quite a bit.

We spotted another boat on the horizon so Dad decided to get in touch via VHF. It was an American boat with two young kids onboard. They said that they had come across a Thai long tail fishing boat adrift at sea and they were now towing it behind their boat on a long line. They hadn't decided what to do with it yet but it was reducing their speed by a good few knots an hour.

We sailed through the Nicobar Islands without stopping off.

On day four of the passage we had a bit of a strange weather system go over us. The wind turned to the west and we were now getting over 30 knots on the nose. It rained and there was lots of thunder and lightning around and over the top of us, it was rather scary. We started to worry about being hit by lightning as we had a few near misses just off the back of the boat. The whole night we tried to avoid this large squally system but every direction we turned it just stayed over the top of us. It was starting to freak us out and we just couldn't get away from it. We could make the large weather system out on the radar and we noticed patches of clear so we headed towards that but it just seemed to keep following us. With strong head winds we weren't making good progress at all so we were forced to put the engine on quite high revs to make any speed.

The engine then started playing up from being run for so long. The revs kept dying right down on it. Dad thought it might be dirty fuel in the filters again so we kept our eye on the filters throughout the night. The last time this happened we were coming into Bali and the engine died completely and we had to be towed in. We really didn't want to go through that again as it was a stressful experience. Just the sound of the revs dying on the engine sent chills right through us and we knew that it was only going to get worse and we could possibly lose our engine again. Every time the revs died our hearts sank.

And just when things couldn't get any worse the fan belt driving the water maker broke so we were now unable to produce fresh water onboard. The water maker was driven by the engine and slowly took in seawater from outside, put it through high-speed filters to produce fresh water which slowly tricked into our tanks. Whenever we put the engine on we put the water maker on too to keep the tanks topped up. We used this water to drink, shower and wash the dishes and our clothes in.

The next morning the weather was better and it was nice enough to sail again and fish. Within a few hours we had caught a lovely one metre wahoo which we had freshly cooked for lunch. It was delicious and nice to taste a different fish for a change. That evening we watched "The Green Mile" starring Tom Hanks. I think it had had to be the worst film I had ever seen, it was just horrible.

Chapter 16
Sri Lanka - Land of Tea

16th January 2000

We finally arrived into Galle, Sri Lanka, late afternoon through the marked channel of buoys.

The engine was slowly getting worse but had not quite yet died so we quickly got in and anchored as fast as we could. We started dragging and then the engine cut out completely so we rushed down below to clean out the filters and top them back up with fresh clean fuel. One of the rally organisers came out to the boat to make sure everything was okay and if we needed assistance. We managed to get the engine going again and quickly re-anchored and this time it held.

The rally organiser took us ashore to check in at the local customs and immigration. Customs charged us nearly USD$200 to check the boat in. This was a lot higher than usual and Dad was quite shocked why it was so expensive. Customs then returned to the boat with us to check the boat thoroughly including counting every can of beer and alcohol we had onboard. When you check into a country the captain of the ship has to state how much alcohol you have onboard so I guess they were double checking Dad's figures he had written down on the sign in form were correct. This wasn't such an easy job as we had alcohol scattered all over the boat in different places, some under floorboards, some in cupboards, some under seating. We had to try and remember where it all was. There were times in the past that we lifted up floorboards only to find bottles of pop that had been down there for years which we had totally forgotten about.

Not even Australia had counted every can and bottle we had so it came as a bit of a shock. Luckily Dad hadn't fibbed on the figures he had put down so customs were happy.

Guess who we spotted in the anchorage? It was our English friends from the concrete boat. We girls were jumping for joy when we spotted them.

17th January 2000

Our first job today was to sort the fuel and engine problem out. Dad was convinced that we had a fuel bug parasite which turned the fuel into gunk, clogging up the filters. We completely emptied out the 250 gallon fuel tank, which was a rather smelly and messy job, and cleaned the inside of it thoroughly. Then we put new clean fuel back into the tanks and then tried out the engine. It was just in time because one of our friends nearby decided to up anchor, ripping ours out on the way, and hitting into Rainbow Spirit. Their anchor was hooked on our chain for a while and they had

Dad cleaning the fuel filter out.

difficulty getting it off. They couldn't navigate away from us and instead were blown right on top of us. Now we were dragging and drifting. After a bit of panicking they finally freed themselves so we had to up-anchor and quickly move before we hit the yacht behind.

We then went on to fix the water maker fan belt so we could make water again…yay. When all that was done we gave the boat a good clean inside and out as it had got quite messy during passage.

Galle was a mixture of colonial buildings and ruins. We went to check out a nearby fort and bartered with some local men who were selling some very old coins. We spotted a man playing music on his flute pipe while his pet snake rose from a pot in front of him. I'm not sure the snake wanted to dance though as the man kept nudging it with a stick.

Most of the rally boats left to go on organised island excursions but this time we decided to save a little money and book it ourselves through some locals. We found two suitable guys, one was the tour guide and the other the driver.

We packed our bags, secured the boat and clambered into their mini bus. They took us through many beautiful rice and tea fields. We came across a tea factory that gave us a tour of their tea farm and showed us the tea production process from the picking to the sorting and drying and to the tea bags. At the end we were able to sample some of the lovely tea we had just learnt about and ended up buying several boxes of tea leaves.

We were taken to some very large temples that had large Buddha statues inside and out. At the Temple of the Tooth we had to hire sarongs to enter as it was a sacred place that did not allow skin to be showed. We were all dressed like yachties in shorts and sleeveless tops so we all had to cover up. Outside one of the temples was a large elephant in chains, moving back and forth constantly staring at the floor. He looked rather unhappy and we felt quite sorry for him as it looked like he had been chained up for years as his legs were red raw where the chains had been.

We went to the elephant orphanage where they had gathered baby elephants together and were bottle feeding them. It was a little like a circus act and it was a little upsetting because they were all chained up.

We then watched a large group of adult elephants work some of the tree plantations. Where we would have used diggers in the UK, the Sri Lankan people used elephants to do some of the heavy work. This was quite normal for them. Later in the day the elephants were taken down to the local river to bathe. They actually seemed happy washing themselves in the water, rolling around and being scrubbed by some of the staff.

Spices were grown in Sri Lanka and we visited a park in Candy where you could learn about the different spices, herbs and oils and then buy lotions and potions made from the fresh ingredients there. At the end of the tour we were given some yummy herbal wine to try. I'm guessing it couldn't have been alcoholic because we were all drinking it, even Corrie.

One of the many tea plantations.   *Some local children of Sri Lanka.*

Later that evening we went to a dance show called Dances of Sri Lanka and it was really good. The headgear and outfits were quite magnificent.

The scenery on the island was beautiful and unspoilt, but we were quite shocked by how many people and children were begging at the side of the road. There was a lot of poverty on the island. We had some spare Coke cans lying around the minibus so one day when we came across two children at the side of the road Dad gave them a few dollars and a can of Coke each. They seemed chuffed with that. When we could, we tried to buy from the local stalls at the side of the road that sold fruit, snacks, veges and a cow's curd type yoghurt which tasted quite nice when you mixed it with honey. The cow curd came in brown handmade pottery so we got to keep the pots.

One morning we took a very early morning safari trip in an open top four-wheel drive vehicle to the Bundala National Park. We saw lots of local bird life and wild elephants with babies. The babies were so small and adorable. It was nice to see them in the wild after seeing them chained up at the orphanage.

A mummy and baby elephant in the wild

24th January 2000

It was our last day in Sri Lanka and we spent it on a local beach with our British friends off the concrete boat. It was funny how we kept bumping into these boats every few months, so it was lovely to see them again and catch up. Their parents kindly treated us girls to lunch and ice-cream while we were out with them. When we retuned back to the anchorage they gave us several bags of British gossip magazines to take back to our boat to read. This may not have seemed a big deal to most people, but us girls, and even Dad, liked reading them. This would keep us entertained for weeks so we were very grateful.

Samantha Saunders

My Round the World Journal

Chapter 17
Magical Maldives

27*th* January 2000

It was only 430 miles and a three-day passage to Male, the capital of the Maldives. The weather was really good so we did lots of schoolwork on the way.

The Maldives were made up of a double chain of around 26 atolls with more than 1000 islands. With an average ground level of only 1.5 metres above sea level it was the lowest lying country in the world.

When we arrived we entered with another rally boat which had their lovely large spinnaker out so we took some photos of them sailing past. Their spinnaker had a large pig on it, it was Pumba from the Lion King, so we thought it was quite amusing.

We anchored between Vilingili Island and Male in 35 metres of water. We could have anchored in shallower water but there was a big swell coming in and we didn't feel like rolling around the whole night.

Just before nightfall the coastguard came around and told us to move into safer waters. Along with seven other rally boats, we upped anchor in the dark and headed towards a lagoon a few miles away. We really didn't have detailed charts for the area and it became quite unsafe to navigate without daylight so we turned around and re-anchored in the same place.

28th January 2000

As soon as the sun was up customs came onboard to check us in and then we upped anchor and sailed to Vilingili anchorage. As soon as the anchor had gone down we jumped overboard to take a swim. The water was really clean and clear, you could see straight to the bottom.

29th January 2000

We caught a little ferry into the capital of Male this morning. We looked around the local shops and asked around for used phone cards. Many of them wanted money for them as they were really rare, but we managed to get more than 30 cards from shop staff and didn't have to pay anything. One of the shops told us to contact a well-known card collector on island so we met up with him and swopped addresses. He was keen to keep in touch and swop cards through the mail. The town was fairly built up and as it was only about 1 mile across and very flat it was easy to get around by foot.

After a day of shopping and buying supplies from the local supermarket in town we caught the ferry back to the boat where we decided to decorate the dinghy. Dani and I took out permanent markers and decorated it in sea life. We painted starfish, octopuses, seahorses and fish all in different colours.

That evening we had some very nasty squalls go over, some reached 52 knots at one point. We had forgotten to strap the dinghy down on deck and the wind was jerking it around so we were forced to go up in the middle of the night in the wind and rain to strap it down. It's a good job it was tied on with at least one line when the wind started else we may have lost it.

30th January 2000

This morning we moved around to Laguna Beach Resort where Dani and I continued with our drawings on the dinghy. This was a very special place. The water was crystal clean and the beach had the whitest, cleanest sand. The snorkelling was really good too.

After reading through some books I came across the following facts about the islands of the Maldives which I thought were quite interesting.

1. Only one hotel/resort can be built per island
2. Each resort can only cover 20 percent of each island
3. The buildings can't be higher than the tallest palm tree
4. All shark fishing is banned in the Maldives
5. All turtles are protected and all turtle products are banned.

Guhlee Island was close by so we went to check it out and managed to pick up some more cards there. There were so many coral heads in the anchorage that it took us quite a while to untangle and free the chain. We must have spun around a few times in the night because the chain was double wrapped around some of them. The only way to clearly see what you were doing was to have someone with their head in the water over the side of the dinghy telling Dad which way to move the boat. Luckily it was shallow and clear enough to see the chain below.

We spent another week in the Maldives doing lots of swimming, snorkelling and admiring the beautiful scenery. These islands and beaches were simply stunning.

Samantha Saunders

Chapter 18

Keeping an eye out for Pirates

11th February 2000

We set off from the Maldives with a few of the rally boats heading across the Arabian Sea, passing through the Gulf of Aden. It was just over 2000 miles so was a couple of weeks' sailing and was probably the most unsafe area to sail through due to pirates in the area. We were all super nervous about the crossing and none of the boats had weapons onboard to defend themselves if we ever got into trouble. Dad was concerned about having three young daughters onboard if a fishing boat ever boarded us.

We kept in close contact with all the rally boats several times a day via the VHF radio. We weren't allowed to give out our position in case a pirate heard and tracked us down, so instead we all had secret points on our charts and gave our positions according to those markers.

We didn't see many boats for the first week of the trip, only the occasional yacht. The seas were fairly calm and we were motoring a fair bit. Our friends were getting very low on fuel from all the motoring and didn't have enough to make landfall so mid-ocean we came alongside and passed some jerry cans of fuel over to them.

Sharing fuel, mid-ocean

In the second week we came across about 20 killer whales and got within a few feet of one that seemed to be asleep in the water. We followed them for ages to get a closer look but they were so fast that we ended up losing them. We had never seen killer whales from the boat before so it was a special day for us all. We didn't even know that they lived in warm waters; we thought they lived in cooler climates.

During the second week, as we got closer to the coast of Africa, we started seeing more boats. Most were fairly small but they still came quite near to check us out. One in particular was larger than the rest and had a number of men onboard. They approached the back of the boat quite quickly as they had a much faster engine than us. As they neared, Dad started to get nervous and made us girls go down below and put big heavy weather gear on. He told us not to come up or to look out the windows in case they saw us staring. The boat was almost alongside us now and Dad was putting the engine on more and more to speed up.

They shouted at us, which we tried to ignore, before realising that they were shouting for cigarettes. We shouted "no cigarettes" as we had none onboard, but they kept shouting back "cigarettes". They were now alongside us. Dad threw them some tinned food and they seemed to be happy with that and shot away. What a relief that was. We were only a few days from land but still not near enough to get help if anything got out of control.

We heard a few times on the radio that fishing boats had been getting close to the other rally boats but none had tried to board or show they were a threat. I think most of them were just very inquisitive.

One of the many fishing boats that came to check us out

During our passage we developed a problem with our exhaust pipe. This was a large thick black pipe, about 3 inches in diameter, which took the fumes from the engine out towards the back of boat under Mum and Dad's bed and then finally outside. It had developed a crack in it and was now leaking fumes into their cabin. Up came the mattresses and wooden boards underneath. Dad located the crack and temporarily covered it up with tape which seemed to do the job.

23rd February 2000

We finally arrived in Djibouti and went straight ashore to have a private briefing with one of the rally organisers about the next leg of the trip…..the dreaded Red Sea. This passage was known for being the toughest part of the rally trip due to the strong headwinds and large seas that would be on our nose the whole way.

The rally organiser had also brought some mail out for us from the UK so that kept us all occupied for a while.

As well as receiving our regular mail, we also collected a large Fedex parcel sent out by my granddad in the UK which was full of schoolwork, more mail and sweets. Dad had to pay £80 to have it released which was a bit of a shock but there was nothing we could do about it. There wasn't even anything valuable in it so we were unsure why we had to pay to get it cleared. After that we spent the day reading letters and eating sweets. It was so nice to have mail from family and friends as in those days it was the only method of contact other than a pay phone which was way too expensive to use.

We didn't venture ashore much here apart from going to briefings at the yacht club, looking for a new exhaust pipe and stocking up with supplies from the local supermarket.

We waited a few days for the weather to calm a bit as it was blowing strong out at sea. We had 1200 miles to go to reach Eilat in Israel, at the top of the Red Sea, and we would have about 30 knots on our nose if we left now.

Some people just said get on with it and go out into the bad weather and get the awful passage done and over with. Other rally boats decided to wait it out in Djibouti and leave when the weather died down a little. We decided to stay a few more days too.

Chapter 19
Conquering the Red Sea

27th February 2000

After a couple of extra days of waiting the wind died down very slightly and we headed out to sea. On the way out we passed some very strange looking dolphins that had odd shaped noses that seemed to be flat. Maybe they were porpoises and not dolphins.

After a day of sailing the wind and tide soon turned on the nose so we were forced to put our engine on. Our friend's engine wouldn't start at all so they were now forced to tack up and down to get into the next safe anchorage. We wanted to stay close and tried to do the same so we spent the whole day hard tacking into the wind. We only managed to cover 40-50 miles in one day. Normally we would travel at least 150. When we neared landfall we towed our friends in the last bit. We pulled into a sheltered bay off Centre Peak Island about 25 miles off the East coast of Yemen. It was a very small, dry and barren looking island with not much on it at all. The whole landscape was brown with tall vertical cliffs surrounding the anchorage. It wasn't long before we noticed the top of cliffs were dotted with people. They were looking down on us to see what was going on, and on taking a closer look with the binoculars we noticed they were in army uniform and were carrying machine guns. We were with two other rally boats so at least we weren't alone. The other boat managed to get his engine started again and we all agreed we would set of first thing in the morning.

Jazair Az Zubayr Island, Yemen

1st March 2000

When we woke the next morning there was a crowd of locals gathered on the hill waving their arms and whistling. They shot a gun off which made everyone a little worried. They continued shouting and we all decided that some of us should go ashore and meet them. Dad went with two of the captains from the other boats and my little sister Corrie. They filled a goodie bag up to give them. This included tinned food, cigarettes, pencils, crayons and other bits and bobs. They seemed fairly pleased with their gifts and shared them amongst themselves. We counted around 17 people ashore. Most were armed with machine guns so it was a little nerve-wracking making contact.

After Dad returned we were all keen to set off but we decided to check in on the morning net organised by the rally over the VHF first. Just as we were about to lift anchor a customs boat came zooming into the anchorage wanting to check out each yacht. They checked our passports and one of them took a good look around all of the boats. They told us we could stay for a couple of days then before they left they asked if we had any cigarettes. Unfortunately with no smokers between us and having just given our only packet to the people ashore, we had none to give them so they left with nothing.

An hour later we finally set off and headed in a northerly direction. It wasn't long before we were hit by the bad weather again. We immediately started to tack across the channel avoiding the oncoming waves. At the current speed we were going it would take us three times longer than usual to get to Eilat and we had only just started the trip. The sailing was very rough and visibility wasn't the best. There were so many ships around that we kept having to change course to avoid them.

During the nights there were even more ships. We were only managing about 3-4 knots and the large tankers, who were doing at least 15-20, soon crept up on us within a few minutes, so we had to pay very close attention to the radar at all times. The radar allowed us to mark the ships with a line and then track it moving. If it continued down the same line and got nearer to us, it meant that we would hit it so one of us would have to

A number of ships on the radar, all within 2 miles

change course. We could usually track ships up to 20 miles or so away, but with these large seas it was harder for the radar to pick them up, so sometimes the ships disappeared altogether off radar, leaving you a bit blind. Sometimes ships just appeared on the radar from nowhere and we literally only had a minute or two to change course and quickly get out of their way. It was pretty stressful when this happened.

2nd March 2000

We had another night and day of tacking the channel. We were now only managing to cover around 45 miles per day. We tried taking all the sails in and motoring hard into the waves and wind a few times, but with the engine on full revs we only managed to do around 2 knots over the ground. I think we constantly had a knot or two of current against us which wasn't helping at all. It also made it nearly impossible to stand up inside due to feeling sick. It was so bumpy going head-on into the waves and the hull of the boat made a loud bang each time it hit another one. It was just far too uncomfortable, so each time we were forced to tack again. We were all getting rather tired and fed-up by now. We were not enjoying this one bit. It was impossible to cook anything below so we succumbed to eating pot noodles. If we went down below the only thing you could do was sleep as it was too rough to even stay standing inside. You were thrown around like a rag doll.

3rd March 2000

We had now lost sight of the other two rally boats we were travelling with but were still in radio contact. It was Jen's 20th birthday today so we sang happy birthday to her over the radio to help take our mind off the dreadful weather.

That evening the furling gear broke again like it did going into Bali. The circlip had come off from inside the furling gear causing the sail to unravel and come out in full. We now had no way of taking any sail in to reef, so in more than 30 knots of wind we were forced to go on deck in the middle of the night and pull the sail down carefully so it didn't get stuck. We had had some stitch work done on the sail right where it threaded inside the forestay but this patchwork wasn't so good and sometimes when we took the headsail down or up it jammed, leaving us in a bit of a panic to try and free it. We certainly didn't want this to happen at sea so we needed to take it down slowly and carefully so it wouldn't get stuck. We certainly couldn't do it going into the waves so for a few minutes we did a complete 180 and turned with the wind and waves. Oh my…what a difference it made. It was so quiet and peaceful surfing down the waves with the wind behind. Once the sail was down there was no way we could fold it up in such high winds so we had to quickly stuff it into the forward hatch and into the cabin where Dani and

Corrie slept. We replaced it with a smaller staysail which we pulled up on the inside forestay.

That day the wind ended up dying down so much that we were now unable to sail forcing us to put the motor on again. The waves were still big so it was still a very rough ride but we were now managing to cover about 3 miles per hour towards our destination.

We spotted some very huge and playful dolphins off the boat which cheered us all up. There were only about four this time and they didn't swim off the bow as they usually did. Maybe we were just going far too slow for them or the sound of the loud engine scared them off.

4th March 2000

We had now lost VHF contact with Jen's boat. They were on a slightly smaller, steel boat so went a bit slower than us. We were still in touch with our other friends who were now visible by sight. They were just a few miles behind us and it was nice to know that someone was close by.

We even managed to knuckle down with schoolwork during the day and I was chuffed to finish my English course books for the term.

Later on that afternoon the wind picked back up to about 20 knots, which meant we could put the sails out. We were able to increase our speed, but as the waves were now getting larger by the hour, the engine made no difference to the speed so we turned it off to give it a rest. It was also more peaceful with it off as it was loud inside the boat on such high revs.

As we were now tacking up and down the channel on quite a hard angle, we were leaning right over to the side. I'm not sure how Mum managed it but she was able to cook us pasta dinner even though the boat was leaning so much. It was a very bumpy sail. That night during my watch the wind changed to a worse direction forcing us to now sail due west. We were not really making any progress at all heading north up the Red Sea towards our destination but there was nothing we could do but continue on this course. We couldn't sail east as we were too close to the land on the right and needed to tack to the left.

5*th* March 2000

We had another terrible and stressful day sailing today. First the main sail over the boom above the cockpit broke. The halyard that was holding it up snapped off and it shot up to the top of the mast making the sail fall and become unusable. And just when we thought it couldn't get any worse, we heard the dreadful sound of the revs dying down on the engine. It was a familiar sound that our ears instantly picked up. It made our hearts sink and stress levels rise. Dad came to the conclusion that there was dirty fuel in the filters again. We knew that this was probably only the beginning and the problem would gradually get worse as we used more fuel up towards the bottom of the tanks. We had only just started sailing the Red Sea and there was nowhere we could get help from around here. Luckily we knew what to do for now so every so often we quickly turned the engine off, ran down below, blew and cleaned out the filter pipe, removed and cleaned the filter, put it back in, topped it back up with clean fresh fuel (we didn't want any air getting in the fuel system) then quickly turned the engine back on. All of this was done in a matter of minutes. We were getting faster and faster.

We had heard that around eight rally boats had pulled into the nearby port of Suakin, a very tiny sheltered harbour just south of Port Sudan. They were taking a brief rest and waiting for the weather to get a little better. We decided to do the same and arrived in just before sunset. The landscape and scenery was unbelievable. Everything was a sandy brown colour as the buildings were constructed from coral and they were all now in ruins. Not a tree or any greenery was visible and it looked very bleak. It was surreal, a little like we had entered into a derelict war zone. It looked like everything had been destroyed and was in ruins.

Thousands of years ago Suakin used to be the largest and busiest gated port in Sudan. It was full of wealth and was known as the pearl of the Red Sea. Every building was made of stunning coral and the walls were decorated in detailed wood and stone. But in the 1920s, when the slave trade decreased, the port was no longer needed and it was closed. Trade was moved further up the coast to Port Sudan instead leaving Suakin unused. The port slowly disintegrated along with its coral buildings. Now all that remains are a small population and the remaining ruins, some of which are carefully guarded for the tourist industry.

As soon as we dropped anchor I had to go straight up the mast to untangle and free the halyard that had snapped off the mainsail and was now up the top. The scenery was so surreal and different that I took the camera up with me to get some shots from the top of the mast.

Customs came over to check us in and the agent who came onboard was very professional and friendly. It cost around UDS$150 to check into the country and for his time.

6th March 2000

At 9am we caught a bus into Port Sudan with most of the other yacht crews. En route we passed lots of people and settlements living next to the road. The land was dry and barren and many of the settlements consisted of plastic coverings and old materials as shelter. Some even had a few goats tied up in pens. I guess that was their food supply.

An hour later we got to the town of Port Sudan. It was a buzzing little town with donkeys and camels wandering the streets. It was very poor indeed and was a bit of a culture shock for us all. The supermarkets were very expensive, even for us, so we just bought some fresh fruit and veges. The small local eateries there were dirty and infested with flies but we were all quite hungry by now and the locally cooked food was cheap so we all sat down to eat. The food was actually very good and tasty.

When we returned to the boat we cleaned the fuel tank out again. The bottom was covered in the familiar thick sludge. We replaced it with clean fuel.

At a local café in Suakin

7th March 2000

All of the boats decided to stop one more day so we went to explore the local town of Suakin. Many of the local children there were dressed in rags and a few were begging. We gained a small crowd of followers. I don't think the children saw many tourists in this area so they were curious about who we were. We went to check out the local museum and market before heading back to the boat to do some more repairs.

Dad fixed the furling gear with two other boat captains. It took several attempts as the part he was trying to fix had snapped. They constructed a temporary clip which seemed to do the job. We just hoped it held for the rest of the trip up the Red Sea.

That evening Dad hosted a skippers' meeting onboard Rainbow Spirit to discuss the next leg of the trip. We were nearly half way up the Red Sea by now.

During our passage we had developed a leak in the fresh water pump so when we weren't using water we had to turn it off so it didn't leak water out into the bilge. But that evening we had all forgotten to switch it off and our whole tank of fresh drinking water had now leaked out in to the bilge at the bottom of the boat. We only found out because the bilge alarm went off, but by then it was too late and we had wasted all of our precious drinking water.

Dad went to switch the bilge pump on to empty the water out of the boat only to find that it had packed up too. It was the only way to get the water out of the bilge and probably the only pump that would stop us from sinking if did we ever starting bringing on water. Dad decided to tackle it first thing in the morning as it had to be done before we left.

The local children of Suakin

8th March 2000

Dad managed to fix the fresh water pump and bilge without too much trouble so they were now both up and running. They pulled me up the mast so that I could re-tape around the spreader protectors. These were the plastic stop ends that sat on the end and stopped the sail from rubbing and ripping on their sharp edges. As we had been sailing so close to the wind with all sails pulled in super tight to the boat, the headsail had begun rubbing on them causing them to work loose.

That afternoon we took a bag of clothes and toys ashore for the children and took photos of the ruins. We decided to stay one more night.

9th March 2000

We left early with another four boats. The nasty weather hit us as soon as we came out of the sheltered bay. Here we go again…..The wind and waves got worse during the day and Mum and Corrie became seasick. After being in the calm of the land for a few days they had lost their sea legs.

10th March 2000

Corrie and Mum were still feeling really bad so we decided it was best to make our own food. Dani, Dad and I took turns to do watches while Mum rested. We literally had a couple of minutes to get down below, grab whatever we could get our hands on to eat and return as fast as we could to the cockpit before the queasiness hit us. Our beds or the cockpit were the only two places you could be without feeling sick.

We heard on the radio that one of the other rally boats had blown out their headsail in a freak gust of wind so they were now heading for another port again. Two of the other boats joined them to take shelter and the rest continued on.

11th March 2000

Mum was feeling a little better and was able to come back on deck again but poor Corrie was seriously ill. She was vomiting constantly and each time we tried to get water down her to prevent dehydration she was sick again. She had been vomiting for three days now and we were starting to get worried. She was gagging over and over again but nothing was coming up. She was constantly in tears and we really didn't know what to do. It was far too rough to do schoolwork, so when we weren't on watch we either watched a movie down below or went to bed.

12th March 2000

The bad weather continued throughout the night but during the day it calmed a little and the sun came out. Mum was feeling a little better today so she was able to stay in the galley long enough to cook us a meal. It was nice to eat some proper food instead of a cup a soup or sandwich. Even Corrie was feeling a little better so they must have got their sea legs a little.

We continued along for the next few days, just plodding along and trying to make as much distance as we could. We were still only managing to cover 50-70 miles a day towards our direction due to the strong winds and oncoming waves, but at least we were heading in the right direction.

15th March 2000

After lunch the engine suddenly cut out and wouldn't start. We found that we had trapped air in the system so with the help of a friend giving instructions over the radio. Dad and I bled the system and after a couple of attempts at trying to start the engine, it finally started. Oh my, what a relief it was to finally get it going again.

Our friends on a nearby boat had also developed a problem with their mast. With all the slamming of the boat from going head-on into the waves, the foot of the mast that sat on a metal plate on deck had worked its way loose and had slid a couple of inches to the left. It was gradually getting worse so the captain was worried and suggested going into port.

We decided to head for the nearest port with three other boats to check the engine out properly, take a look at our friends' mast and fill up with fuel, as we were nearly out again. We still had full jerry cans of fuel tied down to the back of the boat, but in these sea conditions there was no way we could empty them into the fuel tank from deck. We would have flooded it with water.

16th March 2000

We anchored in a bay called Sharm Luli off the coast of Egypt. The landscape here was barren and dry. We were desperate for fuel so we went ashore to find some civilisation. We came across a group of soldiers who spoke no English. After 20 minutes or so trying to communicate with our hands they figured out what we were after, they nodded their heads and went off. We assumed that they would return in the morning.

We then got to work on our friends' mast. It was decided that it was best for me to go up and check the rigging for any breakages as I was the lightest and had also been taught what to look out for. I actually found it quite exciting being hoisted up by the captains below. You get such a good view from up there. We then loosened the rigging on each side of the mast and hammered the bottom over so it sat back in its place.

That night Mum and Dad cracked open some wine to chill out. They had found this whole trip very stressful and needed a well-deserved rest.

Late into the evening, we were woken by a huge bang. Dad had had one too many drinks and had accidently walked straight down from the cockpit into the saloon missing every step and hitting the saloon table below. He had hit his eye and leg badly and had split his eyebrow open. Within a matter of minutes his leg had swollen but I'm not sure he knew exactly what was going on or if he could feel anything as he went to bed. We kids were a little worried that maybe he had fractured something.

In the early hours of the morning when it was still pitch black we were woken by the soldier guys shouting from ashore. Our friend off another boat also woke up and dinghied over to see what was going on. They had our fuel ashore and wanted us to collect it and pay them for it. I woke up Dad, who was semi-unconscious and had no idea what was going on. It would have been too dangerous to even try and get him in the dinghy drunk, so I sent him back to bed and got a friend on another boat to help me collect the fuel containers and get them on board.

17th March 2000

The next morning Dad woke wondering why his leg was so swollen and blue and why he had a black eye. He was hung over but was keen to go ashore and collect the fuel. He didn't believe me when I told him we had already collected it in the middle of the night.

Once we had emptied the fuel containers into the boat we left port and believe it or not had hardly any wind. The seas were a lot calmer and we just motored, averaging around 6-7 knots per hour. This was more like it and we were making good progress.

That evening we were still able to motor and put the sails out. There were so many ships to avoid. At one point I had more than 10 on the radar so it kept me on my toes tracking them constantly to make sure we weren't on course for each other. The mainsail decided to break again so we had lost the mainsail for the second time on this passage. It had only been a few days before that we had fixed it so that didn't last long.

As we neared land the seas and wind died down, allowing us to motor even faster.

19th March 2000

Yay, we had finally arrived in Eilat, Israel. At the very top of the Red Sea there were two forks, the left went to the Suez Canal, and the right fork to Eilat. We had arrived just in time for a welcoming party organised by one of the local hotels.

What a relief it was to finally arrive in port. It seemed quite built up with modern shops, hotels and sky rise flats. Before we entered the marina we had to come alongside an old tug so that we could check into the country. The tug had huge big black tyres as fenders and it was leaving thick black marks all over our white hull. Dani and I were not looking forward to having to clean this off. We imagined it would be a right nightmare. As we entered the marina we had to go under a bridge which they had to lift up for us to pass underneath. We girls noticed fairground rides to the starboard side ashore. Some of the rides looked huge. We excitedly jumped up and down on deck, shouting at each other. We couldn't wait to check it out.

We moored stern-to the large dock and opposite was a construction site where they were building some flats or maybe hotels. A couple of doors down was a McDonalds so as soon as we had moored we went to get ice-cream...... Well I think we all deserved it after that trip, don't you?

That night we went to the party ashore organised by a large hotel. There were free nibbles but we had to buy drinks. It was good to see the other rally people and we spent the night swopping Red Sea tales.

While it took us two weeks to sail up the Red Sea due to the bad weather, the funny thing was a couple of boats who had waited out in Djibouti an extra week for the weather to calm, made the trip in around five days. We weren't too amused. What should have taken us five days took us three times as long.

Dad still had his black eye from his fall and lots of the people commented on it. It was a good job he didn't show them his black swollen leg. He joked that Mum had done it, which everyone laughed about.

20th March 2000

We quickly noticed that there was a friendly homeless dog living in the building site opposite us. The builders fed her scraps of food and we were over the moon when one of them introduced us to her very young pups. She had around five puppies and the builders looked out for them, which was nice. They had given her a protected place for her to shelter while the pups grew. They were so young they could barely walk. We ended up calling her Bessy-Boo.

23rd March 2000

We had been feeding Bessy-Boo and her pups every day. She was so friendly towards us that we spent any time we could with her.

After a few days doing jobs on the boat Dani and I went around the rally boats asking if we could clean anything for a bit of pocket money. A lot of boats gave us their dinghies to clean and polish and this time we were careful not to break the floorboards. Another couple gave us their barbecue to clean. It was so filthy that you couldn't see any silver inside.

We scrubbed and scrubbed but the dirt and grime would not shift off the grilling plate. We decided to use acid on it as that seemed to be quite powerful and would probably get the old meat off. We smothered the grate in it and went inside for lunch, but when we returned it was in pieces. The acid had eaten through the small bits of solder holding it all together. We had broken it and it was totally unusable. We were rather anxious about telling them but when we did they told us not to worry as they could fix it. We didn't do any more work for other boats after that as we were too worried about breaking something else.

Dani with Bessy-Boo

26*th* March 2000

Most of the rally boats had gone away on tours to visit Jerusalem and the nearby sites, but the tours were so expensive that Dad decided to leave it. None of us were really religious either so we weren't too fussed. We went to check out the local shops, sites and markets instead.

Yesterday a couple from one of the other boats offered to babysit us, or should I say child mind us, on their boat while Mum and Dad got some alone time together and went out for a romantic meal. They kindly took us out for pizza for dinner then to the fair. After going on some of the rides, we came across a netted area full of tiny trampolines. It was only a few dollars to have a go on for half an hour and we just couldn't wait to get in and jump around. The wife of the couple used to be a trampoline instructor so she spent a while teaching us how to do front flips while she supported us with her hands. We had so much fun, but it was also tiring. Around 8pm we went back to the couple's boat to watch a movie. Dad had organised to pick us up from their boat after they had finished. 9pm came, then 10pm and Dad still hadn't come to collect us. We were all so tired that we ended up falling asleep in their cabin while watching the movie 'Independence Day'.

31st March 2000

Most of the boats were out of fuel from all the motoring we had been doing up the Red Sea. There was no fuel dock around so a fuel tanker was organised to come to the dock and fill each boat up individually. Many of the boats now had the dreaded thick sludge fuel bug like us so were very wary about putting new fuel in their tanks in case it made the problem worse. I think once you had it, it spread quite rapidly to all the fuel like a fungus. We had cleaned our tanks out twice now, had added a chemical which was supposed to kill it off or at least prevent it, and we were still having engine problems with the fuel.

We still had more of the Red Sea to go up yet so this part of the trip wasn't over. We all still had quite a bit of motoring left to do so we had no choice but to all fill up.

1st April 2000

Well it was April Fool's Day today and Dad being the joker he was was thinking of ways he could fool the other boats. We had been having so many problems with fuel recently that he wanted to play a joke on them saying that the fuel we had put in the tanks the day before was contaminated and the fuel lorry was now having to pump it all back out again. This was quite believable and he went one by one down the boats on the dock telling them of the awful news. You should have seen some of their faces. Some people looked so shocked that they were speechless, others were swearing and shouting in anger. Some knew what he was up to and laughed. He told them the truth 10 minutes later and they were so relieved while others were now even angrier.

7*th* April 2000

After checking out of the marina we quickly checked up on Bessy-Boo and her pups, which were all well and walking by now. We then set off out of the marina around 11am and moored alongside the big old tug to check out of customs.

We set off a couple of hours later for the Suez Canal. It was windy, around 30 knots, and it seemed to be increasing. Luckily it was coming from behind us and pushing us from behind as we headed south down the right fork of the Red Sea.

8*th* April 2000

During the night the wind was a constant 35-45 knots and we even recorded a gust of 53 knots on the wind instrument panel on my watch. That was the strongest wind I had been through on the boat. The waves picked up and we started to get waves break against the back of the boat and into the cockpit. We decided it was best to overlap and share watches of four hours on and two hours off between Mum, Dad and me. It was so windy that the Bimini awning above the cockpit ended up tearing.

As we came to bottom of the right hand fork we turned the corner and the weather calmed. We had heard on the radio that the boats ahead were getting hammered with 30-35 knots and large seas so Dad decided that it was best to take shelter in a port that night and so we pulled into Sharm el-Sheikh in Egypt.

We went stern-to the dock with our friends' boat on one side of us and a Turkish boat on the other. We paid an agent there around USD$40 to stop the night and that evening the Turkish boat invited us onboard for tea and biscuits. They showed us around their boat and they had a Play Station onboard so we stayed on and played for a while.

Suddenly the agent came around and shouted at us to get off. We were not allowed to board other yachts as we were officially in transit. He seemed quite angry so we quickly hopped back onto Rainbow Spirit.

9th April 2000

As soon as daylight appeared we set off for Suez. We had no wind to start with but as soon as we turned up the left fork to the top of Suez, we were met with 30 knot head winds. It wasn't quite as rough as other parts of the Red Sea so we didn't think it was too bad.

We were travelling closely with two other yachts. Unfortunately they were both having problems. One had engine problems and the other had ripped their mainsail, causing them to slow down so much that we shot ahead and could no longer see either of them.

We shared watches that night as the amount of ships and unlit oil rigs was awful. We ended up doing five hours on and five hours off with Dani and I sharing a watch and Mum and Dad sharing theirs.

10th April 2000

We motored into the wind all day averaging between 2-3 knots per hour. There weren't too many ships during the day and we kept in sight of four other rally boats. One of them was so tired with only two crew onboard that they made a last minute call to head into a port to take shelter and have a good night's sleep. We were tempted to do the same but really just wanted to finish the trip as fast as we could.

11th April 2000

The wind didn't die down until about 5am and when it did the seas were flat which meant we could now do 6-7 knots. We were making good progress. We heard over the radio from some of the other rally boats that customs ahead were fairly strict and fined you if you had any out of date safety items on board. We checked the date on the life raft. That was okay but the fire extinguishers hadn't been serviced in years. They were just there for an emergency really. We quickly printed out some labels to stick on them showing a newer date.

We arrived at the entrance to Suez at around 11am and a pilot came onboard straightaway. He checked the safety equipment and everything was okay. Phew! We then headed to the fuel dock as we were nearly out of fuel but when we got there the pump didn't work, so instead we moved onto the water dock where they had fresh water. We filled our tanks up and washed all the salt off the boat. It was so nice to get the salt off the deck. Salt becomes tacky and sticky and it also absorbs water so when it's left on deck overnight it becomes damp in the morning. It was also a nightmare for rusting things so the sooner we got it off the better. It only cost USD$4 to give the boat a good wash down and to fill up the tanks with water so Dad was quite chuffed.

We then headed for some moorings. This time we were told to attach both bow and stern to a mooring buoy to keep all of the yachts pointing in the same direction. This was to prevent us from spinning around and hitting each other. What a relief it was to finally complete the Red Sea. One of the worst passages on the trip was now over.

When we checked into some countries you sometimes paid a one-off fee for the boat and all crew onboard while other countries charged per person. Suez was reasonably expensive and charged per crew. Our friends on a nearby boat had four crew onboard but they didn't want to pay the high fees in Suez. Instead, they decided to hide two crew in the toilet onboard, thinking customs wouldn't check there. They were right and they got away with only paying for two crew instead of four. I wonder what would have happened if they got caught?

As we were just in transit for the night and wouldn't be going ashore, we decided that it would be cheaper just to check Mum and Corrie into the country so they could go ashore to pick up some fresh supplies. Poor Mum didn't have such a good experience though as she was hassled quite a lot and found the whole experience quite stressful. She came back quite upset about it all.

Re-fuelling at the dock in Suez

12*th* April 2000

Next part of the trip was the Suez Canal which was the access to the Mediterranean. Some of the rally boats set off that morning but we decided to chill out a bit longer and go to the party ashore hosted for the rally boats by the Egyptian tourist board. There were gifts, raffles, Egyptian belly dancing and very sweet cake. We were given a painting on reed paper, an Egyptian women's head which was surprisingly heavy and a bronze plate. Corrie's raffle ticket got pulled out and she won another bronze plate. The dancing seemed to go on for hours which became a little tiring so we went home before it finished.

13*th* April 2000

We were due to set off this morning but didn't leave as there was a gale on its way and the canal was closed to yachts. Ray, the oldest member of the rally, finally arrived on his boat Lady Rosemary. He was single-handedly sailing up the Red Sea and I think he very nearly gave up. There were days when none of us could reach him on the radio, and times when he wanted to pack it all in, give up and turn around. It was just too much for one man to navigate the boat for days and weeks on end with no rest. He must have been completely exhausted. We were all so worried about him and were so relieved when he finally pulled into Suez.

That evening we decided to organise a welcoming party for him. We baked him a welcoming cake and made a huge welcome poster. We couldn't believe it when we finally saw him. He had lost so much weight that we were all rather shocked, but he was over the moon with the party.

The gale never did hit that night.

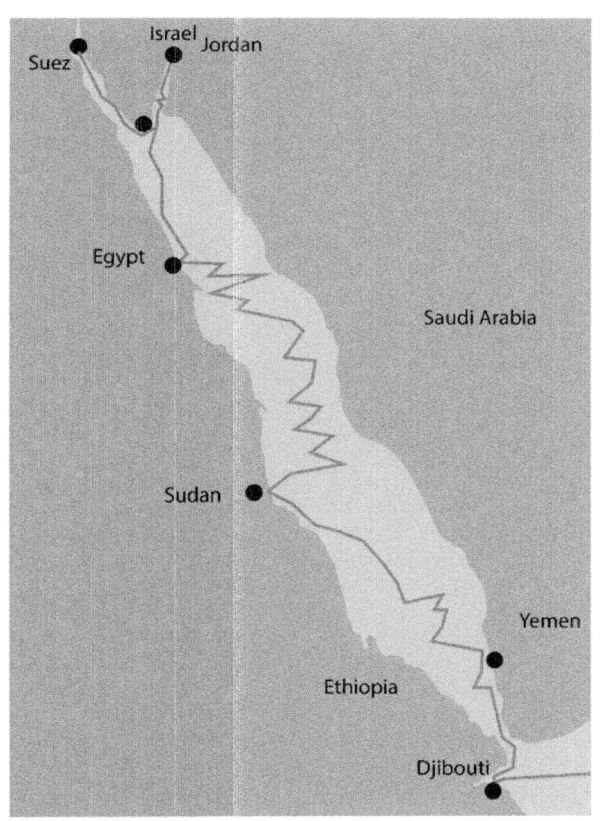

Our route up the Red Sea

Samantha Saunders

My Round the World Journal

Chapter 20

The Suez Canal

14th April 2000

After our pilot had joined the boat at around 11am, we set off and motored through the first part of the Suez Canal to Ismala, the half way point to Port Said. It was a long day and we were nervous as we had heard from the rally organiser that the pilots were known to make you pull over en route and make you hand over cigarettes and food to people ashore. Our friends a few hours ahead confirmed our suspicions were true. They had been rammed by a boat when they hadn't handed over enough cigarettes. Luckily they were a steel boat and it didn't do any damage, they were just all a little shaken. We were anxious throughout the day as we knew that at any time our pilot could pull the boat over. Luckily ours didn't.

We didn't get to Ismala until after dark and we were expecting a boat to come out and pick the pilot up, but no one turned up. We didn't want him sleeping onboard so Dad made us pump up the dinghy which was rolled up and stored away on the deck. This was the last thing we wanted to be doing at this time of night but we eventually got the dinghy in the water and dropped the pilot off onshore. We were all so tired that we went straight to bed afterwards.

Passing one of the many container ships in the Suez Canal

15th *April 2000*

In the morning we went to collect our pilot from shore, along with our friends' pilot who jumped onboard too. I guess no transport had been organised for them and we were the only ones with a pumped up dinghy.

The other rally yacht came alongside us so their pilot could jump ship on to their boat and we continued through the canal all day.

The Suez Canal was rather boring and barren. Not much civilisation around or greenery, just lots of flat, dry land. We passed a very high bridge being built in the distance. We guessed it must have been for a new motorway that they were building. We shared the channel with traffic travelling the Suez Canal, so it was interesting to pass so close to the large tankers in calm conditions. There were no locks like panama, just a very wide canal.

At the end of the trip the pilot cheekily asked for a tip so we gave him around USD$15 and 20 packets of cigarettes. We thought that this would be enough and he would be happy, but he asked for more. He was sent home with no extras as we had nothing left. There was no anchorage here to stop at so we just continued sailing towards Crete, which was a large Greek island in the Mediterranean.

The weather was lovely and we sailed through the night.

16th April 2000

We had to turn the engine on at around 9am as the wind died down and we could no longer sail. We motored the whole day and Dani kindly took an extra watch for me in the morning so I could crack on with some extra schoolwork. She was ahead with hers.

During the day we noticed a bird had landed on the boat. He was so tired that we were able to bring him down below to feed him.

Samantha Saunders

Chapter 21
Sailing the Med

18th April 2000

We continued motoring the rest of the way towards Crete and pulled in to Agios Nikolaos at around 6pm. We moored up, hooked up to water and electric then jumped ship onto another rally boat to have some drinks. It was great to be in the Med again, back to civilisation and away from dangerous waters with pirates.

That evening we met up for a meal with my grandparents who had flown out from the UK to see us. How lovely it was to see them again. It had been more than eighteen months since we had last seen then and they came with post and goodie bags full of sweets and chocolate.

Corrie decided to go back with them that night and sleep in the apartment they were renting.

19th April 2000

In the morning we gave the boat a good wash down and good clean on the inside then Nan and Granddad joined us for lunch onboard with Corrie. We spent the rest of the day catching up and getting lots of cuddles.

25th April 2000

We waved goodbye to Nan and Granddad today. They had already been in Crete for a week and we had seen them every day. They even came to two of the rally parties that were hosted for the boats. One was in a large Greek restaurant where there was Greek dancing and the smashing of plates. We had also hired a car and spent a few days touring around the island with them and sightseeing.

Crete was the largest most populated of the Greek Islands.

Agios Nikolaos Harbour

30th April 2000

Dad had organised a 48 km bike ride for the rally today, so we got up early, picked up our bikes and after being taken in a van to a location, 22 of us set off. We went up hills and down hills and we passed through many villages. We stopped off at one for lunch and had the most amazing Greek salad. One of the men on the rally was a little too old to cycle so he hired a large motorbike instead and drove alongside us. Throughout the day we spread out, with the slower ones at the back. Mum wasn't so good at cycling up hills so she ended up pushing her bike some of the way. Corrie stayed behind to keep her company. We had such a smashing day although we were rather tired and had sore legs when we had finished.

1st May 2000

Pinch, punch, first of the month. It was Monday today and we had a tidying up day with a couple of boat jobs. One of the rally men came over to get some photos of the bike ride the day before from Dad's computer.

2nd May 2000

Can you believe that they have a Makro in Crete! Makro is a large warehouse type store that sells food, furniture, clothes, pretty much anything in bulk and at wholesale prices. The Makro back home was two storeys and it took you a good few hours to get around. The Crete store wasn't quite as big as the one at home but we still were able to stock up on quite a bit of food.

3rd May 2000

Dad was getting itchy feet to get on a bike again so we went back to the cycle shop and hired two more bikes. We put them on the back of our hire car and drove around all day along the south coast of Crete, cycling on the downhills when we could. We were going to stay overnight in a hotel but as we were still close to the marina we ended up driving back there and sleeping on Rainbow Spirit that night.

4th May 2000

We set off early to do some more touring in the car. We also checked out a couple of hotels to see whether they would be suitable to stay the night but they were very grotty. In the end we managed to find a family room in Agia Galini for about USD$70 which was still a bit pricy for us but was a lot nicer that the others. The harbour was very pretty with all the traditional fishing boats and white washed buildings overlooking the harbour. We watched the local fisherman come in for a while and took lots of family shots in the pretty surroundings.

5th May 2000

We set off from the hotel and did a circular route over the mountains. Me and Dad cycled a bit of the way but it was such a cold day that it made it really unpleasant. We ate sandwiches for lunch which Mum had made that morning to take with us, and that evening we returned to the Sky City Hotel again in Agia Galini.

6th May 2000

We left the hotel and drove west along the south coast to Sfakia where we spent the night in a lovely village. It wasn't as built up here so it was really peaceful. There were only a few hotels and houses dotted around the village but there were still a small number of restaurants and shops bordering a nice grey sand beach. Dad and I used the bikes a couple of times during the day on some downhills.

7th May 2000

We checked out of the hotel and slowly made our way along the north coast of Crete towards Hania. We did the Gorge walk, which was around 15 miles and took around three hours. Dad had read about the walk in a British newspaper that Granddad had bought out with him. We just happened to be near it so we went to check it out. After the walk Dad got a lift in a local pick-up truck that took him back up the hill to fetch the car. He then picked the rest of us up and we spent a night there.

8th May 2000

We thought we'd better head back to the boat again so we completed our road trip by slowly following the north coast back to Agios Nikolaos Marina.

20th May 2000

It was time to set off and after a quick trip to the local shops to stock up on some fresh supplies, we headed out just after lunch heading west along the north of Crete. We pulled into a remote island called Sia, and anchored in the first bay by ourselves. This very flat island was covered in birds but there were no trees visible, only very low lying shrubs. It reminded me of the dry and barren Yemen Island we had pulled into up the Red Sea. At night it was pitch black as there were no lights at all on the island. It was similar to being at sea.

21st May 2000

After a peaceful night alone in the anchorage we set off very early and motored 60 miles up the coast to Rethymnon. Here we dropped anchor and went stern-to a large and newly built quay, next to another four yachts. The harbour was huge and the town was lovely so we ate out in a local restaurant that night.

22nd May 2000

We were supposed to leave Crete today for Malta, but the weather forecast had turned bad so we decided to stay in the harbour instead. We spent the whole morning walking around the beautiful town in Rethymnon and checking out some local ruins. After going back to the boat for a few hours to rest and have a bite to eat, we set out again to spend the afternoon ashore.

23rd May 2000

I still had a bit of Greek money left over which needed spending so Dad walked me into town around 7.30am so I could spend my last few pennies. Not many shops were open this early except a couple of newsagents and cafés.

We then set sail for Malta and motored the next few days as there was no wind at all.

26th May 2000

Yesterday we passed a very large turtle in the water. It was swimming rather strangely so we motored over to check it out. It looked like it was dying, it had some sort of rubbish or line attached to its back flipper. Every time we got near it, it tried to swim away. Unfortunately there was nothing we could do to help it except leave it in peace.

Injured turtle that we found

Today the wind was calm in the morning, and then around lunch time all of sudden it got really windy and was gusting 30 knots from behind. How bizarre that was, with such a sudden change of weather. The wind then suddenly calmed down then picked back up all over again. There was no cloud or rain to warn us, it was just an invisible gust.

We then came across another small turtle. This one tried to swim to the back of the boat but we were going far too fast for it to catch up. The wind slowly increased and we were now getting nearly 40-knot gusts so we took all the sails in and sailed bare-polled throughout the night. We were still averaging 5-6 knots with no sails at all. We had the wind and waves from behind pushing us.

28th May 2000

We stuck with our normal watches during the night and had two house martin birds land on the boat. They looked so tired so we put them in a box and gave them water. When the sun eventually came up, we noticed that the waves were huge. The weather forecast ahead in Malta was force 6-7.

We had no choice but to go through a dangerous passage as we entered Valletta Harbour in Malta. It wasn't at all sheltered. We tried to take our time but the wind and waves were pushing us so fast we couldn't go any slower than about 7-8 knots. We eventually made it through the channel safely.

We arrived in around 7.30am and went stern-to the dock, next to our friends' boat. A few hours later some more of our friends came in so we helped them with their lines. The weather didn't ease and it became very rough where we were moored so our friends up-anchored and left to find somewhere more suitable. We decided to remain where we were.

The island, although very built up, didn't have much greenery at all, just lots of very sandy looking brown buildings making the landscape look quite drab.

An English agent came to the boat and took us to customs to check us in. It was still quite early in the day when we had finished so we went to check out the local town. There were lots of chandleries dotted everywhere and Dad's eyes lit up when he saw them. He had a good thorough look in them all. It had been the first place for a while where you could buy quality boat parts. The streets and city were dirty, just like a typical city really.

We went to a local chippy for lunch but the exchange rate was so bad for the British pound that the chips alone cost more than £15.

29th May 2000

Today we had the horrid job of servicing the heads which were the toilets on the boat. We had been having problems with the toilets for a while, especially the toilets we girls were sharing up the bow of the boat. Every time the toilet was used it had to be hand pumped out by a handle and then fresh water pumped back in. It seemed to be getting harder to pump as time went on and the toilet seemed to be getting clogged more often when someone used it. After servicing the toilet itself, everything seemed fine in that area, so we investigated the pipes. The normal 1.5 inch outlet pipe had developed a build-up of a solid calcium-like substance on the inside of it, reducing the width to about 0.5 inches. No wonder the toilet kept blocking. We removed the 4 metre pipes over the next two days from both toilets and bent and banged them on the concrete dock to slowly break up the build-up which we thought might be from the salt water. It was not the nicest job and quite smelly, but it had to be done. After about half a day we weren't getting too far, this stuff was like rock. To our relief, Dad decided it was easier to go down the local chandlery and purchase new pipes. After we fitted them the toilet flushed like new, it was so easy to hand pump the water in and out.

1st June 2000

We were stern-to the dock as the tide changed quite a bit throughout the day and we didn't want to keep adjusting our lines. It was still very rough and windy so we pulled the boat forwards a little so we didn't crash into the dock behind. This made it very difficult to get off the back of the boat as we were now far away from the dock. Anyone that wanted to get off needed to get somebody else to pull the back of the boat in with the line while they quickly jumped ashore before the boat went back out again.

Dad decided we needed a boarding ladder which could be lifted up at night so people didn't jump onboard from the dock. We went to the local chandleries to take a look but they cost a fortune to buy, so instead Dad bought some nice quality timber, paint and some non-slip strips. He spent the next day making it and it looked really good. We couldn't wait to try it out. He gave it a last coat of paint but it wasn't quite dry enough to bring onboard so he left it on the dock overnight.

When we woke in the morning it was gone. Someone had stolen it, probably for the wood, maybe even another yachtie. Dad was gutted as he had to start it all over again. This time he bought a ladder and put some planks on top with the non-slip strips. He didn't bother painting it this time but it did the job nicely and was quite a bit lighter than the one that was stolen.

Dad's second attempt at the boarding ladder

3rd June 2000

It was Corrie's 11th birthday and we walked around town looking for some rollerblades. Dani and I had had ours since Australia but Corrie didn't have her own pair yet. She had used ours a few times but they were just too big on her. We couldn't find any cheap sports shops like we did in Oz, but instead we came across a professional skate shop that sold designer brands. We found some top quality Roces rollerblades that were more than twice the price of ours. Corrie absolutely loved them and you could see what good quality they were, so Dad bought them for her birthday. She couldn't wait to try them out and as soon as we got back to the boat we all went rollerblading together. It was great that all three of us could now rollerblade together.

That evening we invited Ray over for a nice home cooked dinner. He had so much energy. He may have been more than 70 but he still ran around like a 20-year-old. He even had a go on the rollerblades and he was better than any of us. He seemed to have no fear of anything so we were slightly nervous that he would fall in the water as he was zooming up and down the dock so fast.

4th June 2000

We left Valletta Harbour for Pantelleria, a small island just off Italy. It was around 150 miles north-west so we took an overnighter. We had no wind on the trip so ended up motoring the whole way again.

5th June 2000

As we neared land, a weather forecast came in. It was predicting a bad weather system reaching us in another 24 hours or so. Dad made the call of passing by Pantelleria and going straight to Sardinia which would give us more shelter.

6th June 2000

Throughout the day the weather got worse and worse and as we slowed down, our ETA into Sardinia got later and later. The wind picked up and the waves got bigger but we managed to get in around 9pm, just before it got dark. The bottom must have been very weedy because it took us several attempts before the anchor held. The bay was huge and we couldn't see a house in sight. There certainly wasn't anywhere we could check in. When the sun went down normally you could see the shoreline dotted with lights, but not this bay, everything was pitch black as soon as the sun went down. It didn't feel like we were anywhere near land.

7th June 2000

It was rainy, windy and horrible today as the weather system passed over the top of us. We spent the whole day inside keeping dry. Another two rally boats had pulled into shelter and they came onboard for tea. Our computer had been on its last legs for a while and so Steve the computer guy fixed it for us and installed the latest version of Windows 98.

Later in the day we thought we were dragging so we re-anchored to make sure we were securely in place.

8th June 2000

The bad weather had now passed and we set off early for Puerto Colom in Majorca in the Balearic Islands off Spain. I think when these weather systems pass over they take the wind with them because we were stuck with no wind again and we motored the whole day and night. One good thing about not having any wind was that it meant that the watches were easy and those who were sleeping slept well. It also meant that Mum didn't get seasick while preparing food in the galley.

9th June 2000

Well, we didn't quite make the good progress overnight as we had hoped to. Our ETA at this rate would mean that we would arrive into Majorca in the dark, which we really didn't want to do. Instead we headed to the nearer Balearic island of Minorca and just made it in in time before dark. We stopped in Puerto Mahon, the capital of Minorca.

Mum making tea in the Galley

10th June 2000

Well the good weather didn't last long because another gale was now nearing us. The weather got worse over the next few days so we decided to stay put. At one point the winds were so strong that boats were dragging all around us. Even the proper yachties were dragging. Normally it's the charter boats which don't really know what they are doing and don't dig their anchor in properly.

We weren't totally surrounded by live-aboards though. One idiotic charter boat started dragging and instead of picking his anchor up properly and re-anchoring, he just decided to motor around the bay with his anchor down. He did this for a good 20 minutes and we don't know how he managed to miss catching somebody else's chain. He finally dug in and moored right next to us within a few metres. We couldn't believe it but I think the winds were so strong they didn't want to bother getting wet in the rain and lift the anchor up properly. Dad was not amused as they were now so close. We put fenders out in case they hit us.

It was raining constantly and was windy with poor visibility so we didn't venture ashore to go sightseeing Instead Mum and Dad made a quick trip in to check into the country. We girls hoped that our neighbour didn't drag again while Mum and Dad were onshore so we anxiously looked out of the saloon windows while they were gone.

When the weather improved we went ashore to check it out. It was a pretty place, quite built up but at the same time there was lots of greenery on the island. It really did feel like we were in Spain with all the colourful Mediterranean buildings and restaurants. Mahon seemed quite a well-to-do place with lovely old architecture that attracted lots of superyachts and large powerboats along the harbour front. Fancy cafes and boutiques overlooked them.

It felt good to be in a European place again, somewhere we knew was safe to sail around.

We stayed for a couple of nights until the gale passed over.

13th June 2000

We refuelled today from the local fuel dock. It was late in the day and they were closing so we asked the staff there if we could possibly spend the night there and leave first thing in the morning. They were rather miserable about it and told us to leave, even though we had just paid to fill up our tanks and had also been paying to anchor every night since we had arrived.

We went back to anchor again and as soon as it was dug in properly, we put the anchor stopper on but it suddenly snapped. The anchor stopper was a bit of elasticated rope. You attached one end to the anchor chain with a shackle and the other end to the deck of the boat. You could then release the chain and the stopper would take the weight off the anchor. This line had many advantages. Firstly when the boat swung around in the middle of the night it was a lot quieter than the chain clunking around on deck. It also took pressure off the windless, which could sometimes have a mind of its own and release chain randomly. If that ever happened the chain would eventually run out allowing the boat to drift away. This time as I was putting the anchor stopper on it suddenly gave way, losing the stainless shackle on the end into the water. We temporary fixed a line on for the night and Dad made a new even stronger and better stopper the next day. We had been using this same stopper for a few years so I guess it was time that we upgraded.

14th June 2000

We set off for Majorca today. It was only the next island away so it didn't take too long to get there. We dropped the hook and had lunch. We then heard on the radio that some of the rally boats were in San Antonia on the next island of Ibiza. It had been a while since we had seen anyone we knew so we upped anchor and headed straight there.

A few hours later we pulled into a very full and busy marina that had the trickiest and tightest berths we had seen. We had to practically push ourselves in between the yachts to get in and it was such a squeeze.

15th June 2000

What a busy little place this was, or should I say a fairly large place. There were so many tourists and youngsters around and it was buzzing with cafés, shops, hotels and restaurants. The pontoons and boardwalk around the port were huge and were made of nice clean, smooth concrete so of course we girls got our blades on and spent as much time as we could rollerblading around the promenades.

We were due to leave a few days later but Mum and Dad had fallen out and neither would say when we were leaving. Luckily they were friends again by that evening and we all went out to check out the nightlife. We saw lots of scantily clad youngsters, holiday reps, street performers and sports bars. We ended up having a drink in an English bar called Charlie's Place where we had some yummy English fish and chips. What a treat that was as we didn't get chips very often. A football match was on, England verses Germany, so we stopped to watch the end and England beat Germany 1-0 so everyone in the bar was quite chuffed. It did start getting a bit rowdy and loud for us girls so we were glad when Dad said it was time to leave.

18th June 2000

It was Father's Day today so we got up early to give Dad his presents and to pick him up an English newspaper. We then set off for the Spanish mainland towards Cartagena.

En route we noticed a large black object coming up behind us. We had no clue what it could be, maybe a pirate boat being all black. It was quickly nearing us and was much faster than us. It was such a bizarre shape that we had no idea what it could be. We knew it wasn't

The submarine through the binoculars

a yacht as it had no mast or sails. We quickly got the binoculars out and realised it was a large submarine. It was rather eerie as it slowly rose from the water.

Cartagena was a relaxing city to walk around. There were lots of archaeological sites, historical buildings, museums and shops. It was Spain's main naval base so there were lots of naval items dotted around the city and port. We came across one submarine out on show and it was interesting to see it up close and appreciate the sheer size of it. Over the years so many different cultures had built in the city and had left their mark on it. The buildings were impressive and historic.

We stayed a few nights and then slowly made our way west along the south coast of Spain. We had to arrive in Gibraltar for the end of the rally a week later and we didn't want to miss the celebration.

26th June 2000

It was the last day of the rally and we made our way into Gibraltar. All of the boats arrived in at the same time. We had been given the time of 2pm weeks before so we knew when we had to be there by. We all sailed in together with our rally flags up. There were horns sounding, people clapping ashore, random people welcoming us in and some onlookers who probably wondered what on earth was going on.

All of the boats came in to the marina all at once so there was bit of a traffic jam when we came into dock. A few of us got into a pickle as we were all supposed to go stern-to the dock and attach our bows to a morning buoy allocated to that particular berth. Some yachts accidently took other peoples lines, others got them caught up in their props, some didn't even have a spare mooring so had to move somewhere else. But we all eventually moored. As soon as we were secure we jumped onto the dock where there were TV crews filming us and champagne was thrust into our hands. The Gibraltar TV wanted to interview the boats with families on board and Dad was happy to do it. It was little nerve racking to be on TV but luckily we kids only had to say a couple of words about our schooling onboard.

For the next week we attended activities and get-togethers every evening organised for all the yachts. There were parties, visits to the boats by the governor and a trip to the Government reception where we were each presented with gifts by the Minister of Tourism. Each boat was presented with a Blue Water Rally plaque with their boat's name on and the map of the trip. The youngsters got a bag of goodies with stickers, clothes, hats and a really nice penknife each engraved with the Blue Water Rally name.

Being interviewed by Gibraltar TV

There was a trip to some of the Gibraltar lower caves which were amazing. I couldn't quite believe that these amazing places existed underground. The stalagmites and stalactites were really fascinating to see. In one of the caves we had to climb up and down rope ladders and pass over thin ledges surrounded by water. Dani accidently slipped into the water when she lost her balance. She was not amused but we thought it was hilarious as she then had to complete the rest of the tour in wet clothes.

The very last evening was a party organised by the rally yachts. It was called 'the survivors party' and was hosted on the pontoon right behind where we were all moored. We all had to dress up in something that we had bought while sailing around. We all brought food and there was lots of cake, so much in fact that Dad ended up getting into a friendly cake fight with another rally yacht. What a mess they made but we managed to get lots of funny photos.

A few days later it was time to say goodbye to the rally organisers who had flow out to Gibraltar with their wives. The yachts presented them with some gifts to say thank you for organising the Blue Water Rally and for all the support they gave to the boats during our circumnavigation.

Gibraltar Airport was literally 50 metres away from the marina so we could hear and see every plane land and take off. We were right next to the runway. When the rally organiser's plane took off some of the captains from the yachts all stood on the end of the pontoon and did moonies. We never knew if they saw it or not but it was rather funny to watch.

2nd July 2000

One by one the remaining rally yachts left Gibraltar. Some were staying in the Med, some were returning to their home country, others were going west across the Atlantic and some were even sailing back to the UK.

Now that the rally had come to an end we were all going our own separate ways and we couldn't help but feel sad. As each boat pulled out of the marina we waved them off knowing that we would probably never see them again. Some people were crying, to them we had become a big family over the couple of years we had been travelling together and now we had to say goodbye for good.

One morning we were waving yet another rally yacht goodbye as they headed out of the marina when all of a sudden they stopped dead in their path. They had hit the bottom of the marina and were unable to move anywhere. They then had to sit in the entrance of the marina for two hours while the tide raised them off the bottom.

Yachts have keels on the bottom of the hull. This is for structural support for the boat but it also keeps them on course and acts as a weight to help keep the boat upright. Depending on the size of the boat the keels could be between 1–3 metres deep. So the draught of the boats (how much of the yacht stuck below water level) could be anywhere between 2–4 metres. Rainbow Spirit's draught was about three metres so this meant that we would hit bottom when the water was three metres deep or less. As tides went up and down in the marina you could have anywhere between 0.5 and 3 metres below you while you were moored.

Once the boats had all gone their separate ways we stayed on a bit longer in Gibraltar. It was strange, but also great being able to walk up the high street and shop in British stores such as Top Shop and Dorothy Perkins and then to be able to pay in UK pounds. It had been so long since we had used the currency that if felt strange holding it again. There was even a Tesco supermarket next to the marina. How wonderful it was to be able to go in and buy English items such as Branston pickle, Heinz baked beans, Cadbury creme eggs, Bisto gravy after being without them for so long. We girls were so happy to be there, it felt like we were back in the UK again.

We made quite a few trips around Gibraltar, sightseeing and meeting the many monkeys they had there. Then our great aunt flew out for a few weeks so we headed back towards the Med.

Over the next few weeks we pottered along the south coast of Spain, stopping in quaint little marinas on the way. Estepona was quite a large and built up city full of facilities and beach resorts dotted along its large beach.

One day we pulled into a tiny little marina called Marina del Este and plugged into shore power there to charge up the boat batteries. All of a sudden we heard a loud bang and smoke started coming out from behind one of the saloon seats, where the inverter box was. It was burning and we got the extinguisher ready just in case. There must have been a fault with the shore power because it blew up when we plugged in to power. This meant we could no longer use the plugs onboard and would have to wait for a new inverter to be shipped out from the UK.

We told the marina office but they didn't want to take responsibility and wouldn't help. Luckily we had boat insurance so was able to claim off that. A few days later a new modern and more powerful inverter was installed and we were on our way again.

We were heading further east up the coast when the weather started to pick up. We were all feeling queasy and we really didn't want our great aunt to go through bad weather so we made a last minute decision to pull into a port called Almerimar. This was quite a large marina overlooked by high-rise holiday apartments.

As soon as we had moored up, we noticed a girl rollerblading around so we went to join her. She was a bubbly English girl who lived permanently on her parents' boat in the Marina. It was a large steel boat that her parents took out on charters. Over the next few days she introduced us to more of her friends, including two 15-year-old lads, Paul from England and a French lad. Paul lived on the hard with his parents, sister and their dog. They lived on a large powerboat which their parents were re-fitting. We got invited onboard and couldn't get over the size of it. It was two storeys, with the parents' quarters up the back of the boat and the kids' quarters up the front. The cabins each had their own double bed and bathroom. There was so much room it was more like a small house than a boat. After a few days Paul introduced us to his other two mates who were 17, a couple of years older than me. One was from Belgium and he spoke five different languages fluently, and the other was Dean from England. They both lived on their boats with their parents in the marina. Dean was really good on his rollerblades, doing jumps and tricks. He was also rather handsome and I developed a bit of a crush on him during the weeks we were there, so any spare time we had I went round to his boat to see what he was up to.

There seemed to be lots of boats that lived in the marina permanently, some had been there for years already. I guess because it was a large marina and a bit of a holiday spot full of other live-a-boards, near to large supermarkets, clubs, bars, shops, restaurants and even a shopping mall a 10-minute drive away, it had something for everyone. We were in Almerimar for a few weeks so we spent most of our evenings hanging out with the other kids. The marina was a bit scruffy in parts due to all the building work that were going on, but to be honest we had such a fabulous time because it was the first time we could spend quality time with youngsters for more than a few days and we made really good friends. We really didn't want to leave at all.

10th August 2000

We waved goodbye to our aunt at the airport and set off from Almerimar towards Majorca, a two-day sail away. We had head winds for most of the way so we had no choice but to motor into the wind. Luckily the seas were nice and calm so it wasn't too bad. We saw loads of shooting stars on the night watches as there was no cloud.

12th August 2000

This morning we motored passed Ibiza, the most westerly Balearic Island before pulling into Palma in Majorca. We were planning to pull straight into the marina there but they didn't have a single space for a boat. I guess we should have booked in advance. That had never happened before so we had to anchor out in the bay instead.

Dad spotted another Oyster boat at anchor. It was a 66-foot boat and we went over for a chat. They came over for a drink that evening.

A couple of days later we were finally able to move into the marina and Dani and my best friends flew out from the UK. They were joining the boat for two weeks while we sailed around the Balearics.

Palma was a busy town and reasonably large in size. It had a very wide promenade surrounding the water's edge which had a special path just for rollerbladers. That was the first time we had seen that so every day we rollerbladed down to the local mall to browse the shops. Palma also had a large department store called El Corte Ingles. We spent hours there trying on fancy clothes and dresses for fun and taking photos. We eventually got told to get out of the shop as we weren't buying anything.

When our two friends first arrived at the airport, there were people handing out lilos to tourists. The lilos were of Siemens mobile phones and came in a range of colours. Between us we were given about eight. We couldn't believe it so the next few days we went back and pretended we were tourists again and sure enough we were given more lilos. At the end we had about 25 between us. Luckily they came flat packed so we were able to store them under the floorboards on the boat.

We spent the next few weeks sailing around Majorca and Ibiza with the girls. It was a bit over crowded and Corrie had to move to the saloon, but we all got into a routine with jobs and tidying up each day so the boat didn't get in too much of a mess.

One of our favourite places was Formentera, an island just off Ibiza. The water was crystal blue and so clear and the beach was covered in white sand. The water was like getting into a warm bath. We anchored quite close to shore so could see the clean sandy bottom easily.

26th August 2000

Today we left for Magaluf. The town was buzzing with people when we got there and the beaches were covered in lots of very sunburnt tourists, many of whom had those mobile lilos. It took several attempts to anchor as the bottom was weedy. Even when we did finally hold Dad still wasn't 100 percent happy with it. That evening we went out to check out the local bars. We had some nice traditional English fish and chips and Dad told our friends if they sang karaoke, he would treat them to their meal. So both girls bravely got up on stage and sang a couple of songs. They weren't too bad either.

Dad woke up in the early hours on the morning saying we were dragging so we shot out of bed, upped-anchor and went back to Palma. This time we moored alongside the promenade wall, which was only about USD$15 for the night but we were unable to plug into electricity. The batteries were getting a little low and that evening we wanted to watch a movie on the TV we had in the saloon. We did have an emergency generator which one of the lads had helped fix in Almerimar a few weeks before. So we got it out on deck, got is started and plugged the TV in. All of a sudden the TV made a loud pop and blew up. The inside of it caught fire so Dad quickly pulled it out of the cupboard, ran upstairs onto deck and put it on the dock. Bummer, now we had no TV. It was one of those TVs that had a video player in the bottom and there was still a rental video in it. We didn't want to be fined for not returning it so we tried to get it out. We even plugged it back into power to see if it would work. Nope, it was totally dead and it was stuck inside. We had to pay USD$15 in fines for not returning the video.

30th August 2000

Our two friends had left now and quite a few things needed fixing on board so we pulled into the marina next door. We had lots of people come onboard that day to repair things. The fridge needed fixing as it wasn't cooling down; the inverter needed something done to it and the bow-thruster, which was an open sided propeller in the bow of the boat, had burnt out and broken. Another guy came onboard to look at the gantry as one of the gantry legs had a problem. And just when we thought we couldn't get any more people onboard more people arrived to take the sails away to be repaired. The sails were in desperate need of some new patches and stitching.

1st September 2000

We had finished our schoolwork for the year weeks ago so we concentrated on jobs for a few days while we were on land. We sanded down the dinghy oars which hadn't been painted since we got them. All the varnish had now peeled off so we re-varnished them. The Bimini (the awning over the cockpit) was leaking water so we re-waterproofed it by soaking it in a bucket of chemicals. Three men came onboard to take the bow-thruster out. It was stored in the forward cabin in the hull of the boat under the bed and mattresses. We took that out and then all the rope and sails which were stored under the bed, followed by more floorboards until we finally got to the bow-thruster motor which was protected by a metal grate. It was a right mission getting it out and as the forward cabin was tiny everything had to be brought into the saloon. The boat became a real mess.

During the evenings, we girls rollerbladed up to the local mall which was around 15 minutes away. We loved the rollerblade paths and it felt so safe. For Dani's birthday, Dad had bought her some new brakes, wheels and new ball bearings for her rollerblades. Instead of getting a new pair we upgraded her current ones because she loved them so much. Her blades were now twice as fast as mine so now it was a real effort keeping up with her every time we went out together. I did try her blades on but they were way too fast and I felt unsafe so I stuck with mine instead.

Each night we stayed out later and later in the mall. There was one particular clothing shop called Fishbone which we thought was really cool. It was also very cheap so every time we went to the mall we came back with something small from there. One night we lost track of time and got back around 10.20pm. It was already dark but luckily Mum and Dad were cool about it. I think they enjoyed having the boat to themselves for a bit.

7th September 2000

For the last week we had been waiting for the fixed parts to be returned back to the boat. Unfortunately they couldn't fix the bow-thruster. Dad was frustrated about this because he used it nearly every time we came into a marina, and in the Med there were lots of marinas.

The sails were returned and as there was no wind we quickly put them up and rolled them in. You certainly couldn't put the sails up when it was windy so today was the perfect day.

We then headed to Palma Nova just around the corner. When we got in we pulled in a lovely sheltered bay but in the middle of the night the wind did a 180 sending big rollers into the bay, and causing us to pull out our anchor. It was pitch black and just far too rough to re-anchor. It was like we were motoring into waves as the boat was bobbing up and down so much. Dad made the decision to do an overnighter straight to Formentera. It was very pleasant sail as the wind was behind us.

8th September 2000

To our surprise, one of the rally boats was in the anchorage, so it was lovely to see some familiar faces again. We had heard there were some mud pools ashore so we went to check them out. There were several to choose from and they were really easy to float in. We covered ourselves from head to toe in mud, we couldn't stop giggling. There was no way

Dad was going to let us go back on to the boat like this so we washed it all off in the sea before getting in the dinghy.

Dani and I went ashore to see if we could rollerblade into town to pick up some food but there weren't any smooth surfaces, only sand, so Mum and Dad dinghied ashore to pick up some supplies instead.

14th September 2000

We sailed back to the coast of Spain, spending a night in Cartagena again as we quite liked it there. We then went on to Almerimar. We were so happy about this as we got to see all of our friends on the boats again, and I got to see Dean.

We spent a week in Almerimar and spent any spare time we could hanging out with our friends. It was really quite sad to leave again. It was the first place we were able to have proper friends really but we had to get back to Gibraltar again.

24th September 2000

We got in to Gibraltar quite early and moored in the same place we were before when the rally boats were there. We noticed that three other boats were in with youngsters onboard including the Belgian lad from Almerimar. Our other friend Paul from Almerimar came to see us on the pontoon. He had left his boat there and was travelling around in a campervan with his parents. They were stocking up on British food to take back with them to Spain and were parked in the Tesco carpark.

Over the next week we prepared the boat to leave for the Canaries before heading across the Atlantic again for the second time. We had to go back there so we could start building on the land that Dad had bought there a few years earlier.

Over the years we had been living on the boat we had collected quite a bit of stuff, mostly spare items that we were advised to buy for the circumnavigation such as a second dinghy and emergency rudder. We had never really needed them so Dad wanted to get some weight off the boat and decided to sell them. We cleaned everything up and took some nice quality photos so he could put an ad in one of the yachting magazines. Someone bought the whole lot as a job lot so we boxed everything up to ship back to the UK. There were 16 large boxes in total, which we took to the local airport to post.

4th October 2000

It was time to set sail for Madeira. We did a last minute shop for fresh supplies from the local Tesco and they had a special offer on Cadbury creme egg packs. They were 60 percent off as they were close to their sell by date. Dad worked out that if we each had one every few days for the next couple of months that we needed more than 200 eggs. They were only 10p each so he bought hundreds of them. There was so many that when he put them in a cupboard hidden away in his cabin that they were overflowing. I think he was keeping an eye on them in case we pinched any, ha ha.

So with our 200 Cadbury creme eggs we left Gibraltar for Madeira. We were instantly hit by thick fog, so bad that you couldn't see more than a few hundred metres in front of us. We had a very near miss with a fishing boat that appeared from nowhere, so we started using our horns to warn other boats we were around.

A few hours later the fog cleared and we made good progress. We hadn't been through fog before in the boat.

Samantha Saunders

Chapter 22
Madeira

8*th* Oct 2000

We had a great three days sailing to Madeira where we anchored off the island of Port Santo. It was a mountainous, rocky and volcanic looking island. It was dry and barren and it reminded me of the Galapagos Islands. We checked in and customs didn't charge anything, they just wanted all yachts to pay around USD$8 per night to stay there. I think quite a few yachts missed out on Madeira due to another lot of checking in fees so I think they had now waived this fee to encourage yachts to pass through more often.

While we were checking in, out of the customs office window we noticed a go-kart course. It looked great fun so as soon as we had dealt with customs and the boat was legally checked in, we went to check it out.

9th October 2000

It was Mum's birthday today so we girls got up super early and decorated the saloon for her. We took a cup of tea in to her cabin around 8am, along with a large bowl of Angel Delight with a candle. We didn't have time to make a cake so Angel Delight was the next best thing. She scoffed the whole lot down though so she must have enjoyed it.

We then went ashore and hired a car to have a drive around the island. Porto Santo was a small, rugged looking island with a long white sand beach along the whole length of the island. It was very unspoilt, with only a few hotels and restaurants and not much to do at all really. It was more of a relaxing destination for tourists.

10th October 2000

We had heard that there was some nasty weather with up to 60-knot gusts on our way and the staff ashore advised us that it was best to moor up to their mooring buoys instead. We attached the bow to two separate mornings and the stern to a mooring each side. We had never moored like this but were reasonably happy that they would hold. We doubled our lines up just in case any rubbed through and broke in the night.

That evening Dad and Dani dinghied ashore and cycled to the local shops on the foldaway bikes to pick up a paper and some fresh bread. Throughout the night we didn't sleep much because we had consistent heavy rain and 30-knot winds, but luckily the wind wasn't as bad as we thought we were going to get.

14th October 2000

When we first arrived here we noticed that the harbour walls were covered in boat paintings. As we had some wall paints onboard we spent a couple of afternoons painting Rainbow Spirit, the boat name and our names. It looked quite good afterwards. It was interesting reading some of the other paintings around though. Some had been there for over 15 years. They must have used really good paint. I wondered how long ours would last and added the date to it.

We didn't get back to the boat until around 4pm and quickly packed our bags as we were catching the 6pm ferry to Madeira. It was a large liner that came in and it took a good three hours to reach Madeira. When we got in we went straight to an apartment that Mum and Dad had booked. Corrie and I slept on a pull out sofa bed and my gosh it was uncomfortable.

Dani painting the harbour wall

15th October 2000

We went to explore Funchal town, which was the capital of Madeira and fairly built up. We came across a modern looking hairdressers so mum booked us all in to get our hair cut. Afterwards we came across a large cinema and went to watch a movie called 'Space Cowboys'. This was the first time we had been to the cinema with Mum and Dad so it was a bit of a treat.

Over the next few days we did a bit of an island tour in a hired car. Some of the scenery was stunning and the cliff edges and steep mountains were so high. Mum really didn't like heights at all and Dad liked to play her up by purposely driving close to the edge. It was starting to make us all feel a little nervous in the back. The height of the drop off the side of the roads was unbelievable. I'm not surprised there weren't more crashes here as there were no barriers to stop you from going over.

21st October 2000

Today the marina called Mum and Dad to tell them that there was a big swell coming in to the harbour and the boat was constantly swinging back and forth. They were worried about it getting damaged while we were away. Mum and Dad took the next ferry back to Porto Santo and gave us USD$30 each so we could spend the day shopping. We were happy with this and all took a while browsing the shops deciding on what we could buy. I ended up buying some nice O'Neil sandals. I was really happy with them. Dani bought some skateboarding Vans trainers.

Mum and Dad returned that evening and we girls walked over to the ferry dock to meet them. We were a little worried at first because the boat never arrived when it should have but an hour later we saw it coming in. What a relief that we weren't spending the night on Madeira by ourselves.

Dad had said the boat's fairleads (brackets where the rope goes through on deck, so it doesn't rub) had been badly damaged. They were bent and some had even snapped off. He was glad he went back to secure the boat and check she was okay.

Over the next few days we stayed in various hotels on the island, some were so high up the mountain that we were above the clouds. There were lots of cliff edge walks around but Mum really didn't like the heights at all so we ended up not doing too many.

At the second highest point in Madeira we stayed in this stunning hotel which was very nice but also expensive. There were walks around it but the weather was so windy that we thought it was best to stay inside in the warm. They had a games room there and Dani and I started to play each other at pool. After a couple of nights we actually got quite good that the hotel staff joined in with us. It's amazing how much we improved from playing for several days.

27th October 2000

It was our last day on Madeira and we bought some tools for the boat from the large tool shops there before catching the ferry back to Porto Santo.

When we got back we noticed the tiniest yacht we had ever seen moored up. It can't have been more than about four metres long. They were obviously crossing the Atlantic like us and we couldn't believe that they would attempt it in such a small boat. You couldn't stand up in it. We thought it was rough on Rainbow Spirit and she was around 13 metres. We couldn't imagine being on a four-metre boat.

The small boat we came across, probably heading across the Atlantic

28th October 2000

It was quite strange waking up on Rainbow Spirit after being in hotel beds for two weeks. We had a nice lie-in this morning and didn't get up until around 10.30am. We needed some fresh bread and food supplies from shore, so Mum, Dad and I took a hike into town. We ended up buying a bit too much to carry back so Dad decided to hire a scooter from a local shop there.

29th October 2000

We still had the hired scooter so Dad and Dani went off exploring in the morning and came across a walk we could do. They told us to catch a taxi to where they were so we could all do the walk. We gave the taxi a time to pick us back up and we started on the walk.

It was a super clear day and the views were really impressive. A few hours later after the walk, Dad and Dani made their way back down to town on the hired scooter and me, Mum and Corrie waited patiently at the top for the taxi to come back to pick us again.

It then started raining and the wind picked up. We got wet and cold and after half an hour of waiting the taxi still hadn't shown up so we decided to start walking instead. We had got about halfway down the hill and the taxi still hadn't come to pick us up so we flagged down another one. When we finally saw Dad he told us that he had just been told that the clocks had been put back an hour. So our taxi wasn't late after all, we were just early. We still owed the taxi for taking us up in the first place so went to find him so we could pay him what we owed. We looked but couldn't find him so we were unable to pay.

30th October 2000

Mum and Dad rode into town on the bikes to have another look for the taxi and to pick up The Sunday Times. We surprised them while they were out by tidying up the boat for when they got back. Being a family of five and all living in such a small space, it didn't take long for the boat to become untidy. Dad always used to say that everything needed a place and if it didn't have a place it would always be lying around, so it was easy tidying up, it was just a case of returning everything back to its proper home.

Later that day when Dad was reading the paper he saw that one of our friends had died. A couple that we knew on another boat had been sailing in bad weather when the wife had fallen overboard. They were both very safety conscious onboard and always wore safety lines and jackets, but on this one occasion the wind had picked up and their dinghy needed tying down at the back of the boat. The husband went downstairs briefly to get a more suitable line and when he came back up his wife was in the water. At that time she was only around 10 feet behind the boat so he quickly took the mainsail down but by the time he had turned the boat around, she was nowhere to be seen. She had gone. He searched for three days and nights until the coastguard ordered him to return to land. He never did find her. It was really sad because they were only a few days from finishing their circumnavigation. She was just the loveliest lady when we knew her and she had spent time with us teaching us how to knit just months before.

It was a good reminder how important safety lines were for us onboard when sailing.

5th November 2000

Mum and Dad had been discussing the land and house in Bequia for a few days. The recent walk that we took on the island a few days before had a similar landscape to the building plot so this morning they both went to take the walk again and discuss their next adventure, building a house in the Caribbean.

As it was a Sunday we girls stayed home and watched some movies. We met them ashore in the dinghy before dark to have a meal together at the yacht club but then found out they weren't open on Sundays so we returned to the boat to eat.

7th November 2000

The past couple of days were spent catching up on jobs onboard and doing some well needed cleaning. Dad and I worked well together when it came to the engine so we cleaned and washed it all out underneath as it was covered in greasy oil and grime. Then we tackled the water maker which needed new filters and the fan belt tightened on it. Corrie had the task of cleaning and chroming Dad's foldaway bike. We had three in total, a blue and red one that us girls and mum used and Dad's was an aluminium one which was just an aluminium grey colour.

After we had finished we spent the day cleaning all the windows in Mum and Dad's back cabin, their bathroom windows as well as the galley and workshop windows. This involved stripping them down to nothing, removing them and giving everything a good clean and oil. Wow, it made a huge difference and they looked really good. We then continued on with the rest of the windows.

We moved the boat off the buoys and into the harbour for one night and then the next day we sailed to Madeira where we anchored in a small anchorage called Baia d'Abra.

9th November 2000

Bais d'Abra was quite a historic bay and the plan was to take our metal detector ashore to see what we could find. But this morning the wind had picked up and was now coming into the bay, leaving it unsheltered and unsafe, so we had to leave early. We headed towards Funchal, the capital of Madeira, where we had taken the ferry to a few weeks before.

12th November 2000

We left Funchal Harbour and did an overnighter south towards a very tiny 2 km wide island called Selvagem Grande. It was one of those places that you would never have the opportunity to go to again so Dad thought as we were passing we may as well take a look.

When we arrived we found that the anchorage there was very unsheltered and surrounded by reefs. We didn't have any charts to help us safely navigate in and as the weather wasn't the best we decided it was safer to give it a miss and sail on to Las Palmas in Grand Canaria, which was only another night's sail away.

Chapter 23

The Canaries

14th November 2000

Our ETA was around midday but on approaching landfall, a small coastguard plane suddenly appeared from nowhere and starting doing dives down towards the boat to get our attention. We immediately got on the radio and they told us that we had sailed into a military testing zone and we had to get out quick as there was a danger we could get fired at. They gave us special coordinates to mark on our chart and told us to sail around the outside of the area instead. By the time we took the long route around, we got in a few hours later than expected.

Dad told us that he, Mum and I had now officially crossed the finish line for our circumnavigation, so that was a good feeling of accomplishment. Dani and Corrie still had the Atlantic to cross yet as they weren't with us when we did the Arc Atlantic crossing four years before.

We girls were happy when we arrived in as we quickly spotted our American friends' boat anchored in the bay. We anchored right next to them so were super close.

We spent a couple of weeks in Las Palmas. It was weird being there again just four years later but it was nice to know where all the good supermarkets and shopping malls were to stock up with supplies. It wasn't often we came into a place knowing it already so we had a slight advantage this time. All the Arc boats were in getting ready to set off. This year we weren't joining them though as we were doing the trip alone. We had organised to meet up with a couple of other rally boats in the area which were also going back to the Caribbean again.

Oyster, the boat manufacturers, were also there supporting the Oysters on the Arc and they kindly invited us to the Oyster party they were having. It was a posh do so we all dressed up in our fancy clothes. We girls got to try caviar and canapés for the first time. We were awarded a 'round the world' plaque and we girls were each given a glass ornament shaped as a book with a globe on. It was beautifully presented in a strong navy blue box with a photo of Rainbow Spirit on it. We were really chuffed with our presents.

After the more than 250 Arc boats had left the marina to make their way across the Atlantic, there were now some spare berths so we moored up inside. We were actually quite close to where we moored before on Arc 1996 and I went to have a look to see if I could find the painting I had done those many years before. I couldn't find it so it must have been painted over with another boat's paintings. Dani, Corrie and I decided to paint a fresh one but there wasn't much spare space on the harbour wall so we found a really old one that you could no longer read and painted over that instead. We felt a little guilty doing this but we didn't really have much choice.

During the two weeks that we were in Las Palmas we had come across so many boats with youngsters onboard. Of course we were all going our own ways after a few weeks but we didn't mind, it was nice just hanging out with youngsters of all different ages and nationalities. A few of them had rollerblades and these little fold up scooters that had just come out so we spent quite a few evenings getting together and trying to do tricks. We constructed some ramps and obstacles from old bits of timber and scrap lying around on shore. One of the lads that we met happened to be from an Arc boat. He spoke with a very posh accent and his clothes were very fancy and clean. The rest of us sat around on the kerbside hanging out and chatting but he refused to sit down in case he got his clothes dirty. When we were wandering around collecting bits of wood he also refused to touch them or pick anything up. We thought this was strange but also rather funny.

Samantha Saunders

My Round the World Journal

Chapter 24

The Atlantic Crossing, Round 2.

1st December 2000

Well it was time to make our way towards the very last leg of our round the world trip....The Atlantic Ocean. After a quick trip ashore in the morning for some fresh supplies we made one last stop on the fuel dock to fill up before heading out of the marina blasting our horn.

We had been going for a couple of hours when Dani suddenly started getting these severe stomach cramps. Dad decided it was best to pull into the nearest port to get it checked out before we set off on our 3000-mile journey. If she did have something serious then we certainly wouldn't be able to get help in the middle of the ocean, so we thought it was better to be safe than sorry and find out what on earth was wrong. We pulled into Porto Rico Marina on the coast where Mum took her straight to the local doctors to make sure it wasn't appendicitis or something serious. Luckily the doctor said she had an inflamed organ and not to worry about it which was a relief to hear.

While we were there, we thought we better spend a day checking it out.

3rd *December 2000*

We set off from Porto Rico Marina around 10am towards our first waypoint some 1000 miles away. We decided to put our clocks back one hour and we had no wind at all so we ended up having to motor the whole day and night. Our rally friends, who were also doing the Atlantic at the same time, had got in touch by radio and were about 35 miles behind us.

4th *December 2000*

Another day without any wind so another day of motoring. We caught a lovely 45 inch dorado for dinner, but when we brought it in we noticed another one swimming at its side. It stayed with it right to the last moment, even after we had taken it from the water. That was really sad. We thought it must have been its mate or baby and it was the first time that had ever happened before.

We girls had a really good day of schoolwork because the seas were flat. I managed to finish my physics subject for the term and started my biology course book.

5th *December 2000*

The engine had been on for two days by now so Dad wanted to turn it off and give it a check over. We put the sails out and were able to catch a bit of wind. A couple of hours later, the engine had cooled enough for Dad to check the oil and water and take a quick peek in the engine room. Everything looked fine and so we turned the engine back on again. Within a few minutes the revs were going up and down, up and down, and we could hear the fan belt slipping. Dad quickly shot down below to open up the engine room door to see what was going on and immediately shouted up to us to turn it off.

Water was leaking from the radiator out of a hole over the fan belt. We added more water to the radiator but it just leaked straight back out again through a small pencil sized hole in the side of the engine. The radiator had a hole in it which meant that we would no longer be able to use the engine to motor or charge the batteries. This was not good as we were only a few days into our crossing.

We spent hours thinking of what to do and called up some nearby boats on the radio. One captain suggested using some liquid metal on it and we knew that somewhere on the boat we might have some lying around.

Liquid metal was a two-part chemical that was runny when mixed together and you had a short time to apply it before it set to a hard metal like substance. We eventually found it under one of the floorboards and the use by date had expired a few years before but it was the best we could do. Dad began to sand down the rusted hole and clean it up with his Dremel drill tool. This was a little hand held tool that had an end that spun around which you could fix different attachments to. Some had sandpaper, some metal and some had wire brush attachments. He used the wire brush tool and slowly began sanding the rust away around the hole but all off a sudden he accidentally pierced a second hole. It had just got so much worse as we now we had two holes to deal with.

Dad mixed the liquid metal up and put it over the holes. It needed at least six hours to dry so we couldn't put the engine on that night. Instead we tried to sail and avoided using any unnecessary electricity or water as we didn't know how long we would be without the engine for. Without the engine the only thing putting power into the batteries was the wind generators or the solar panels and we were reliant on the engine to also make our drinking water. We would have enough water to drink on the crossing but would most likely have to bathe in seawater if it came to it as there wouldn't have been enough water to have a shower every day.

There was no wind at all so we just bobbed up and down with a large swell all night. With the current pushing us from behind we were making around 2 knots over the ground.

What a difference this weather was to the first time we did the Atlantic. This time four years ago we were already getting around 30 knots of wind with large seas behind us. We certainly weren't expecting flat seas this time round.

6th December 2000

During the night we watched the other rally boat that had been 35 miles behind us slowly catch us up and overtake us. As soon as the sun came up Dad filled up the radiator again and hesitantly switched on the engine. We ran it for the whole day checking it often and the liquid metal seemed to be doing its job.

7th December 2000

We managed to sail a bit today to give the engine a rest but the wind soon died down again and so the engine went back on. After inspecting the engine Dad found out that somehow salt water was getting into the radiator. This was not good.

8th December 2000

Yay we finally had enough wind to sail properly. We had a constant 15-25 knots behind us so could now turn the engine off. The seas were still pretty flat so we got on with schoolwork while Dad had a day on his computer, writing and designing his latest newsletter to send to friends and family back home.

I also started the first Harry Potter book as Corrie kept saying how good it was. It did take me a while to get into it but now it's quite good.

We heard a boat on the radio that seemed to be coming over loud and clear. We plotted their position and saw that we were more than 60 miles away from each other. The reception must have been so good because the seas were so flat.

During my 6-8pm evening watch I noticed a bright light directly behind us around eight miles away. With such a bright light it must have been a large container ship or maybe even a cruise ship.

9th December 2000

I think we are now getting the proper Atlantic winds we are supposed to get. We managed to sail the whole night and day again averaging 176 mile in the last 24 hours.

On the radio we heard about a Canadian boat that had set off across the Atlantic a few weeks earlier and the dad was now ill onboard with thrombosis in his leg. He was still a few days from shore with a blood clot in his leg and was in agony. We all hoped that he would make it in time. He was so near to landfall, he just needed to hold on for a few more days.

10th December 2000

The Canadians had made good progress and arrived in Barbados today so the dad was now in good medical hands there. What a relief that was to hear over the radio.

We had now been at sea for a week and were about a third way through our trip already.

11th December 2000

Dad turned the engine on around 12.30pm. It hadn't been run in over three days. We charged up all the batteries, filled up the water tanks so we could all have showers and we even made two fresh loaves of bread in our bread maker. Dad continued with his newsletters as we had lots of spare power so used the computer.

I finished my Biology for the term and went onto English.

12th December 2000

I got woken up at 6.45am by a horrible flapping sound in my bed. A few days earlier we had found a large moth onboard which we had named Stinger Bug. We had put it in a container and were feeding it daily. I thought maybe it had escaped and was now in bed with me flying around. I put the light on but couldn't see Stinger. I then noticed a horrible fishy smell and lifted up my blanket. An 11cm long flying fish had come through my hatch and was now moving and flapping around. Dad who was on watch came and got it and threw it overboard. At the same time Mum, who was in the back with the hatch open, had one jump on her. This one was even bigger than mine. What a smell they left all over the sheets and their scales were everywhere. I guess I was going to be washing my bed sheets today.

13th December 2000

Dad reminded us that four years ago today we had just landed in St Lucia on Arc 96. We had also passed our halfway mark across the Atlantic today and Dad gave us some half way gifts. We each had a new magazine to read. I was given the latest Backstreet Boys album which I insisted on playing over the boat's cd player for the rest of the day, Dani had a cd case and Corrie got given a family of Barbie dolls.

We decided to let our pet moth free.

14th December 2000

We turned the engine on for most of the day to charge the batteries, fill up with water and to make two more fresh loaves of bread. Oh my how I love fresh bread from the bread maker, still warm and so soft. Dad spent the day on the computer and couldn't get the printer to work.

15th December 2000

The barometer has been dropping every few hours as a low approached us. This wasn't good news as it meant bad weather was nearing.

We decided to fill the engine radiator with fresh water again as it was slowly becoming more diluted with saltwater. We still had no idea where it was coming in from. The radiator circulates the fresh water around the engine so how on earth could salt water be getting in? There must be a leak somewhere.

I managed to finish my English for the term and was now onto my last subject, Maths, where I began with some Trigonometry lessons.

17th December 2000

As the low approached, the visibility got poorer. On my 4am watch the headsail suddenly ripped across the bottom. There was a good one metre split where the sail had been slapping and flapping around in the wind. We had to take it down and put the smaller yankee sail up on the inside forestay instead. It sailed nicely.

18th December 2000

This morning on Dani's early morning watch she had a large ship come within around three miles of her. On my watch I wasn't so lucky and had non-stop squalls. I was getting over 40-knot gusts when the squalls came over which was a little stressful, but luckily the sails were nicely reefed.

We always reefed the sails before night fell because sometimes when it was dark it was hard to see a squall approaching. During the day you could see them coming from miles away and could prepare for them in time.

The wind was a constant 25-30 knots throughout the day and as the waves got bigger, the seas got rougher. We now only had 527 miles left to go to Saint Lucia. That was less than three days away.

19th December 2000

Dani had finished all of her schoolwork for the term so she had nothing to do so she took on some of Dad's watches while he continued downstairs on the computer working on the newsletters. Our ETA was in two days so we were all really happy that we would soon be on land again.

20th December 2000

We wrote some hand written letters, put them in some empty wine bottles and threw them overboard today. We fished all day and caught another lovely 51-inch dorado. When we got it in we pulled it on deck, removed the squid lure and hook from its mouth and safely left the lure slightly trailing over the back of the boat while we dealt with the fish. All of a sudden a shark shot out of the water from nowhere and grabbed the lure, snapping it off by the metal. We lost the lure, hook and line weight. It all happened so quickly that we were in a bit of shock. Thankfully no one was on the bathing platform at the back of the boat when it happened otherwise the shark would probably have taken them instead. It must have been following the fish when we were bringing it in. We did feel bad for the shark which was now probably swimming around with a hook and weight in its throat.

Chapter 25
Back in the Caribbean

21st December 2000

We were sailing so fast that we really didn't need the engine on but the batteries were getting very low so they needed charging. We put the engine on and were now averaging over 8 knots with the sails out. At this speed our ETA now changed to that evening so we decided to leave the engine on the whole day and try and get in that night.

We made it in at 7pm that evening and anchored off Rodney Bay Marina in Saint Lucia. Our rally friends were already in and they brought a celebratory bottle of champagne over in their dinghy. Dani and Corrie had now officially completed their circumnavigation so we gave them congratulatory hugs.

We slept so well that night. What a relief it was to be finally in but at the same time a little sad that our travelling adventures were now over.

22nd December 2000

We only had a couple of days before it was Christmas so we brought the boat into the sheltered harbour there and moored off a dock just outside of the marina. It was only USD$11 per night including water and electricity so dad booked us in for a week.

January - April 2001

We spent Christmas in Rodney Bay Marina. Mum managed to buy a turkey and some Christmas pudding from the local supermarket. There were no vegetarian alternatives in the Caribbean so I had an omelette instead.

Dad was keen to get back to Bequia to see how overgrown the land was there and to do some clearing. After not really doing much physical activity on the boat at all, a day of clearing the land and burning it left us completely worn out. Our bodies were not used to the exercise.

Over the next few months we lived on Rainbow Spirit off the local beach in Bequia and went up to the land most days clearing and burning. Together we came up with the name of Tropical Hideaway to call the house and property when it was finished.

In April that year we all returned to the UK. It was very bizarre getting off the plane in London and was a bit of a culture shock. There seemed to be so many people and traffic. My granddad and nan were there to greet us. How wonderful it was to see them again.

We soon settled back into school while Mum and Dad planned their next adventure…the building of Tropical Hideaway…...but that's another story.

Chapter 26
A little update

So what are the Mansfields up to now?

After a brief time in the UK finishing off the girls' schooling, the family returned to Bequia to start their five-year building project on Tropical Hideaway, taking on much of the building work themselves. During this time Sam kept an online blog of the build at www.buildinginbequia.com.

The build was completed in 2011 and Martin and Julie now both run it full time as a luxury guesthouse and villa. More information can be found at their website at www.tropicalhideawaybequia.com.

While in Trinidad, Sam ended up bumping into Dean, the lad from Almerimar Marina in Spain who she had a soft spot for. They have been together for more than a decade and are now married. Sam graduated with an Honours Degree in Computing and Design and she now works as a freelance graphics and web designer in New Zealand. You can check out some of her work at www.samidesigns.com.

Dani trained as a holistic therapist and spiritual healer and now works for high profile clients around the world. Her website is www.daniellemansfield.com.

Although Corrie graduated with an Honours Degree in English, she followed in Dani's footsteps and now works as a hostess, masseuse and beautician at resorts and guest houses around the world.